Published by

ATLANTIC

PUBLISHERS & DISTRIBUTORS (P) LTD

7/22, Ansari Road, Darya Ganj, New Delhi-110002
Phones : +91-11-40775252, 40775214, 23273880, 23275880
Fax : +91-11-23285873
Web : www.atlanticbooks.com
E-mail : orders@atlanticbooks.com

Disclaimer

- The author and the publisher have taken every effort to the maximum of their skill, expertise and knowledge to provide correct material in the book. Even then if some mistakes persist in the content of the book, the publisher does not take responsibility for the same. The publisher shall have no liability to any person or entity with respect to any loss or damage caused, or alleged to have been caused directly or indirectly, by the information contained in this book.
- The author has fully tried to follow the copyright law. However, if any work is found to be similar, it is unintentional and the same should not be used as defamatory or to file legal suit against the author.
- If the readers find any mistakes, we shall be grateful to them for pointing out those to us so that these can be corrected in the next edition.
- All disputes are subject to the jurisdiction of Delhi courts only.

Printed & bound in India by Atlantic Print Services

Foreword

Literature of diaspora has gained the attention of readers and academicians. Indo-Caribbean literature too has been revered and studied about for its rootedness in themes and tropes such as kalapani and coolitude. V.S. Naipaul assumes a significant position in Indo-Caribbean literature with his long and prolific literary oeuvre, perceptive travel narratives, and saga-like novels.

Dr. Sonal Sharma's present endeavour is a lucid critical analysis of Naipaul's three travelogues, known as Indian trilogy—*An Area of Darkness, India: A Wounded Civilization,* and *India: A Million Mutinies Now*. It also unpacks valid remarks on the cultural and political commentaries that Naipaul makes. Dr. Sharma's undiluted analytical approach and her insights too are the noteworthy features of the work. Her command over diaspora theory too gets amply evidenced in this book. Tenets of diaspora consciousness including hybridity, cultural dilemma, nostalgia, homeland/host nation paradigm, and identity crisis are effectively located in this well-researched critical study. It indeed is a worthy addition to Diaspora Studies. I recommend this useful critical study to all those who like travel writing, diaspora literature, and Indo-Caribbean culture.

Dr. Dinesh Nair

Diasporic Consciousness in Sir V.S. Naipaul's Indian Trilogy

Sonal Sharma

Preface

V.S. Naipaul is one of those prolific writers who have global repute and recognition. For his versatile genius of insightful writings and originality of concepts, he has been honored with the prestigious Nobel Prize. He holds a place of prominence among the most widely read literary figures in diaspora writings. His prolificacy is enormous and admirable. He is the most admired among Indo-Caribbean writers. His writings exhibit varied aspects—his minute observation, his eye for details, and his concern and sympathy for the poor. He has been one of the finest diasporic writers in English.

Diaspora entails cross-cultural writings, and Naipaul's relationship with India and his Caribbean upbringing get reflected in the cultural canvas of his writings. His relationship with India finds expression in his deep-rooted concern for the land of his forefathers.

Naipaul's creative works include novels, short stories, and non-fiction. His travelogues deal with the leading theme of rootlessness. He feels himself alienated wherever he goes. He considers himself as an Indian in West Indies, a West Indian in England, and a nomadic intellectual in the post-colonial world. His views on India and Indian culture also reveal the complex problem of identity. He has the triple identity. He is a descendent of an Indian Brahmin family originally migrated as an indentured laborer. He is a West Indian by birth and grew up in Trinidad. Finally, he was subsequently an expatriate in London living in a self-chosen exile till his death in 2018. In an attempt to discuss Naipaul's diasporic consciousness, I have kept in mind these three aspects of his identity.

Naipaul has his reputation as a travel writer more than as a novelist. He has written many travelogues. His travelogues, especially three of them on India form Indian Trilogy. They have angered many Indians, particularly sensitive critics.

Naipaul is a global persona. From time to time, he has been awarded for his excellence in the field of literature. Many research works have also been done on his fiction and non-fiction. But, I have refrained from writing excessively on this already much discussed aspect of writing. Instead, I have focused on Naipaul's relationship with India in context of his acclaimed Indian Trilogy.

Naipaul's three books on India, *An Area of Darkness* (1964), *India: A Wounded Civilization* (1977), and *India: A Million Mutinies Now* (1990) which are central to this analysis display his diasporic consciousness.

The title of the book itself defines the scope and purposes of my publication. The work has been divided into six chapters—(i) Introduction, divided into two sub-parts: (a) V.S. Naipaul: The Author in the Making, and (b) Diasporic Writings: An Overview, (ii) The Homeland Nostalgia, (iii) Social Ethos, (iv) Cultural-Cross Currents, (v) The Outsider's Perspective, and (vi) Conclusion.

The first chapter includes V.S. Naipaul's brief biographical sketch and his successful literary career as a cosmopolitan writer. In this chapter, Indian Diasporic writing has also been overviewed. The second chapter deals with the Naipaul's homeland nostalgia and establishes an engagement with the country of his ancestors and traces how his views have been completely changed about the country of his origin. The third chapter records Naipaul's social ethos where he presents a critical analysis of the Indian and the historical degeneration as well as the malpractices prevailing in the society. The fourth chapter discusses the cross-cultural currents that Naipaul faces during his subsequent visits. The fifth chapter presents Naipaul as an outsider in the context of India. In the sixth chapter, I have tried to draw findings and conclusion on the basis of analysis carried out in the preceding chapters. A detailed list of works cited has also been added for further references. I believe that this book will add to the body of Naipaul scholarship and will be handy for the students and researchers of English Studies.

Sonal Sharma

Acknowledgements

First of all I am deeply indebted to my mentor Dr. Dinesh Nair, for helping me one way or the other by offering admirable suggestions at different stages of my work and for motivating me to get the work finished within time. I express my heartfelt sense of gratitude to him for the encouragement throughout the writing of this book.

I acknowledge my deepest indebtedness to all my seniors and colleagues in believing and reminding me the value of this work. For facilitating my literary survey, I express my sincere thanks to all the librarians at British Council Library, New Delhi; Aligarh Muslim University, Aligarh; and Jawaharlal Nehru Library, Mumbai University.

My acknowledgement will remain incomplete if I fail to record my indebtedness to my parents. I find no words to thank them. I whole heartedly dedicate my work to my mentor Dr. Dinesh Nair and my parents Mr. R.L. Gautam (father) and Mrs. Nirmal Gautam (mother). They all are the foundation of my life, without whose blessings this work could not have seen the light of the day.

I am truly obliged to many critics and scholars and my seniors who helped directly or indirectly in forming an opinion expressed in this book. I feel delighted to express my special thanks to my dear husband Mr. Gaurav Sharma who persistently helped me in collecting excerpts, reviews, criticism, and other important material from the very beginning to the end. He has been a great help to me.

Last but not least I acknowledge my heartfelt thankfulness to God for protecting me from the difficulties and problems in pursuit of this work.

Sonal Sharma

Contents

List of Abbreviations

AAD	*An Area of Darkness*
FC	*Finding the Centre*
FDS	*The Five Dollar Smile and Other Stories*
IWC	*India: A Wounded Civilization*
MMC	*India: A Million Mutinies Now*
MP	*The Middle Passage*
MS	*Miguel Street*
RW	*Reading and Writing*

1
Introduction

(a) V.S. Naipaul: The Author in the Making
(b) Diasporic Writings: An Overview

(a) V.S. Naipaul: The Author in the Making

Sir Vidiadhar Surajprasad Naipaul holds a place of eminence among the most celebrated diasporic writers in English. He was born on August 17, 1932 in his maternal grandfather's Indian-style house in Chaguanas, in the Caribbean Island of Trinidad. He was the second child of Seepersad Naipaul and Droapatie Capildeo. His maternal grandfather was a Banares-trained Brahmin who had come to Trinidad on a five-year contract of indentured laborers to work on the sugar plantations and at the end of contract, they were to be given a piece of land or a free passage to India. But after five years, these promises proved to be hollow and they became homeless and penniless.

V.S. Naipaul did not have any knowledge about his father's family. It was only in 1972 that he had come to know about the history of his father's family. Namrata Rathore Mahanta explains how Naipaul gains this: "To Naipaul and his family India was just a far-off dream. He grew up knowing nothing about his father's and very little about his mother's. It was only in 1972 that he got a complete idea of his family history" (Rathore Mahanta 17-18).

Naipaul's idea of India evolved out of the fact of his birth into a Hindu joint family of Trinidad. He grew up in an extended family of which was rigidly bound by Indian customs, traditions, rites and rituals and always tried to guard Indian culture against the dominant culture of the Caribbean. It was not only people but also the domestic articles which were laid down around him to represent the country of his ancestors. One of Naipaul's earliest memories is of gold teeth Nanee and her husband who was the friend of his mother's family. They always spoke Hindi and never tried to learn English. Both husband and wife carried their India with them. Naipaul grandfather had also brought various domestic articles from India. Naipaul explains the cultural value of such articles:

> More than in people, India lay about us in things: in a string bed or two, grimy, tattered, no longer serving any function, never repaired...in plaited straw mats: in innumerable brass vessels; in wooden printing blocks...in drums and one ruined harmonium...in brightly coloured picture of deities on pink lotus or radiant against Himalayan snow; and in all the paraphernalia of the prayer room...the images, the smooth pebbles, the stick of sandalwood. (*AAD* 23-24)

Naipaul's father was a reporter and used to work for *The Trinidad Guardian*. It is after being inspired by his father that he aspired to become a writer. In *Finding the Centre*, Naipaul recalls how in an anthology of poetry which he received from his father at the age of three, his father had written: "To Vidiadhar, from his father. Today you have reached the span of 3 years 10 months and 15 days. And I make this present to you with this counsel in addition. Live up to the estate of man, follow truth, be kind and gentle and trust God" (*FC* 72).

Naipaul owed a sense of deep debt of gratitude to his father and regarded him as the motivating force in his life. In his talk with Nigel Bingham, Naipaul has said: "My father was extremely important in my childhood. Nearly everything I am, I am because of his great link I felt with him" (Joshi 25).

Naipaul did his schooling from Queen's Royal College, in Port of Spain and then at the age of eighteen he moved to the Oxford University on a Trinidad government scholarship by the virtue of his splendid academic performance. Naipaul stayed there for four years and did his graduation in English in 1954. In 1955, he married his classmate Patricia Ann Hale and decided to lead the life of a writer. He secured a position with the BBC in writing and editing for the program called 'Caribbean Voice' until 1960.

Naipaul started his literary career by going back to his childhood days of Trinidad with adequate material in his hands. During this period, he launched his literary career by writing short stories based on his Trinidad memories which were later published as *Miguel Street* (1959). It may be regarded as young Naipaul's homage to Trinidad, the land of his birth and upbringing which he had left at the early age of eighteen in 1950. He describes his life thus: "I began to write, I am afraid for no other than reason because I thought it would be nice to be a writer.... In fact, writing is just a sort of disease, a sickness. It's a form of anguish. It's a despair" (*MS* 22).

When Naipaul took to writing, the terms like 'post-colonialism', 'post-imperialism' and multiculturalism were not so popular. He had to struggle a lot as a writer in London where there was no demand for the serious literature, which could support the writer. Amidst these circumstances he launched his literary career. Hammer quotes Naipaul mentioning his early impulse: "To be a writer was to be a writer of novels and stories. That was how the ambition had come to me, through my anthology and my father's example" (Hammer 51-52).

Naipaul is a well read and widely travelled writer. His non-fictional works are an outcome of his travelling across Third World societies. He has written a lot of non-fiction that comprises travel books, enquiries into history and politics, critical essays and personal essays. He has travelled far and wide and has found different social patterns of life and cultural problems of the newly independent nations. He has observed in his Nobel lecture, "Two Worlds," that for him, all literary forms are equally valuable and his travel books have given him a new way of looking at the world. To him, the travel books were fanciful interlude in the life of a serious writer. His travels have played a vital role in shifting his writings from fiction to non-fiction. Mohit K. Ray remarks: "Naipaul is one of Literature's great travellers and his leading theme of rootlessness, the alienating effects of colonial past on today's post-colonial people has taken him to Africa, South America, India and all over the world—not in search of roots but in search of rootlessness" (Ray vi).

Naipaul's first composed work *Miguel Streets* was published as his third book (composed in 1955 and published in 1959). His first published book was *The Mystic Masseur* released in 1957 which established the theme of displacement of individuals in colonial and post-colonial contexts and the struggle of the writer to create a sense of order from confusing social situation.

Naipaul's second book was *The Suffrage of Elvira* published in 1958. This novel is all about democracy coming to an obscure island of multi-ethnic population and later seems to suggest that in spite of the corrupting influences of democracy, people are getting more conscientious towards their responsibilities, duties and rights.

Miguel Street (1959), a collection of seventeen stories, is a record of the keen observation of the author. The language is a pure Trinidadian English and this novel is written with a concern but with a certain detachment too. Naipaul's next novel *Mr Stone and the Knights Companion* (1963) deals with the theme—the struggle of a weak protagonist to overcome his sense of displacement. His novel *The Mimic Men* (1967) is associated with ancestral theme as well as with different aspects of London life. His fiction, *A Flag on the Island* (1967) is associated is a fine collection of short stories set in the context of West Indies and London. His novel, *In a Free State* (1972) received Booker Prize for him in 1971. His novel *Guerrillas* (1975) is a fictionalized version of an actual political issue, psychological conflict, sexual violence and it also records the final collapse of an already debilitated social order. *A Bend in the River* (1979) also depicts the various socio-cultural, political and economic aspects of Africa. *The Enigma of Arrival* (1987) is classified as fiction. This book is an in-depth self-exploration of Naipaul as a writer with the question of identity at its center. *A Way in the World* (1994) reveals the writer's interaction with history, where he consciously blends history with autobiography and fiction. His novel, *Half a Life* (2001) deals with the predicaments of an immigrant. Naipaul's *Magic Seeds* (2004) is an extension of *Half of Life*.

Naipaul's non-fictional works represent his impressions of the countries he travelled. He discovers in non-fiction a mode of expression complementary to the version of the novels. Naipaul believes that the travel experiences paved his way to discover additional subject matter beyond his childhood memories of Trinidad. Travel has become his means of exploring, examining and revealing the lifestyles in various societies of the Third World through the mode of non-fiction. Naipaul has travelled far and wide and his travel books are an outcome of these journeys.

The Middle Passage (1962), his first book of travel writing is an account of his journey in 1950 from London to his birthplace, Trinidad. For this non-fictional work on Caribbean, Naipaul was accused of criticizing the West Indian population. So this book produced the first major attack for snobbery, arrogance and total lack of empathy. Hence, the Government of Trinidad officially commissioned him. *The Middle Passage* records his impression of five colonial West Indian and Caribbean societies—Trinidad, British Guiana, Surinam, Martinique and Jamaica. Namarata Rathore Mahanta explains the premises of this book: "The book declared that the Middle Passage—the deportation of millions from Africa to the new world as slaves had not been blocked; this passage continued on renewed patterns of mass emigration and thrived on the slavish mentality of the West Indians" (Rathore Mahanta 23).

An Area of Darkness (1964), *India: A Wounded Civilization* (1977) and *India: A Million Mutinies Now* (1990) are Naipaul's full-fledged travel documents on India, which form the famous 'Indian Trilogy.' *An Area of Darkness* (1964) is a semi-autobiographical account of Naipaul's first visit to India which had filled him with hopes and speculations as it was supposed to be, in a way, a return to his roots but unfortunately, this visit gave him shocks and disappointments and the country remained for him 'An Area of Darkness'.

The loss of *EI Dorado* (1969) is the outcome of Naipaul's personal research to recover the unknown history of Trinidad and his own roots as well. This novel explores the motives and realities of the mythical Golden city of *EI Dorado*. It is a masterful study of New World history. This history reveals the barbaric cruelties of slavery and torture in Trinidad.

Naipaul emerges as a keen journalist and a masterly reporter in *An Overcrowded Barracoon* (1972). It is a collection of essays divided into three sections. The first section deals with Naipaul's world as a colony and its implications in the world of Naipaul as a writer. The second section contains his views on India and the third section presents Naipaul's vision and the interpretation of the failure of the colonies from the patterns of 'civilized' and 'primitive'.

India: A Wounded Civilization (1977) is Naipaul's second travelogue on India. He visited India again in 1975 at the time of emergency and wrote this harsh but realistic account of the nation.

The Return of Eva Person with the Killing in Trinidad (1980) is a collection of four essays. It deals with Naipaul's travel experiences in Argentina, Trinidad, and Congo.

Among the Believers (1981) presents Naipaul's observation of the societies of Iran, Pakistan, Malaysia and Indonesia—four non-Arab Islamic countries. No doubt, it is acclaimed as one of the finest travel records by an artist who has been recognized as a 'Modern Master'.

Finding the Centre (1984) is Naipaul's autobiographical attempt in which he tries to trace his literary beginning as a writer. The book consists of two parts: "Prologue to an Autobiography" and "The Crocodiles of Yamoussoukro." The first part accounts his childhood, his family and mainly his father. He remarks, evoking the content of this book: "However creatively on travels, however deep an experience in childhood or middle age, it takes a thought (a shifting of impulse, ideas and references that as one grows older) to understand what one has lived through or where one has been" (*FC* 3). Naipaul has also said that the title of *Finding the Centre*: "...has many meanings—Finding the centre of the narrative, the center of truth of every experience, the philosophical centre for one's belief" (Qtd. Ray xiv).

A Turn in the South (1989) is a record of Naipaul's observations during his travelling to the American South West from North Carolina to Mississippi. Here Naipaul also studies the effects of history on people and on individual lives. *India: A Million Mutinies Now* is Naipaul's third book on India. This book seems a kind of final home coming for Naipaul. It remarks that he: "had succeeded in making a kind of return journey...abolishing the darkness that separated me from my ancestral past" (Qtd. Ray xvii).

Beyond Belief: Islamic Excursion among the Converted Peoples (1998), a sequel to *Among the Believers* is on the theme of Islamic conversion in these non-Arab Islamic countries. The book describes his five-month journey, revisiting four Muslim countries—Iran, Pakistan, Indonesia and Malaysia. Namrata Rathore Mahanta observes how Naipaul continued his engagements with Islamic nations: "He continues with his exploration of these four non-Arab Islamic countries. He sees non-Arab Muslims as peoples whose racial culture stands contested by their religious faith and in the confusion that follows people lose sight of themselves and forget who they are" (Rathore Mahanta 25).

Letters between a Father and Son (1999) is the early correspondence between the author, his father and his sister during the period he left Trinidad. In this book, Naipaul writes about the nobility of his father and his struggle. *Reading and Writing: A Personal Account* (2000) is a short work of non-fiction and it examines critically the strands of history which have shaped and reshaped Naipaul's thoughts and ideas. The book moves through memories of his teenage life that consists his days at Oxford and his earliest attempts at writing. Naipaul observes:

> In my fantasy of begin a writer there had been no idea how I might actually, go about writing a book I suppose—I couldn't be sure that there was a vague notion in the fantasy that once I had done the first other would follow. In those

> early days every new book meant facing the old blackness again.... My writing imagination was like a chalk-scrawled blackboard the end black again. (*RW* 27-28)

Literary Occasions (2004) is yet on another collection of V.S. Naipaul's ten essays. The book is divided into two major sections. The first section is made up of essays in which Naipaul examines how his own writing career and the life events that have influenced it. The second section examines the writing of others including Nirad C. Chaudhuri, Rudyard Kipling and Joseph Conrad. *A Writer's People: Ways of Looking and Feeling* (2007) is Naipaul's another non-fictional work. In this book, he discusses how the work of other writers had affected his own writings.

The Masque of Africa: Glimpse of African Belief is a non-fiction published in 2010. The theme of this work is African belief. Naipaul visits or revisits Uganda, Nigeria, Ghana, The Ivory Coast, Gobon and South Africa and he speaks with a wide range of people from diplomats and royalty, to politicians and businessmen to academicians and medicine men.

Thus, one can see that Naipaul is a prolific writer with unique perspective and insights. He is a cosmopolitan writer. He feels at once an Indian, a West-Indian, a nomadic intellectual and a cosmopolitan subject in the post-colonial world.

In February 1996, Patricia died of cancer. Two months later, he married Nadira Khannum Alvi, a Pakistani journalist. Since Nadira is woman of Islamic origin and he is a man of Brahmanic origin, their marriage has strongly confirmed their cosmopolitan outlook. Naipaul himself admits that Nadira has made him a greater author than he was. A good deal of credit for winning the noble prize in 2001 goes to his wife.

Naipaul is a writer of global repute. He has been awarded many prizes for his fictional works and honored by different organizations for literary achievements. Naipaul has been called 'A master of modern English prose' in the *New York Review* of books and has been awarded numerous literary prize including the John Llewellyn Rhys Prize (1958) for the *Mystic Masseur*, the Somerset Maugham Award (1961) for

Miguel Street, the Hawthornden Prize (1964) for *Mr Stone and the Knights Companion*, the W.H. Smith Literary Award (1968) for the *Mimic Men*, the Booker Prize (1971) for *In a Free State*, the Jerusalem Prize in 1983, and the T.S. Eliot Award (1986) for creative writing. In 1990, he was knighted by Queen Elizabeth II for his services to literature. He is the first recipient of the David Cohen, British Literature Prize for a 'lifetime's achievement by a living British writer' in 1993. Above all, he was the proud recipient of the Noble Prize for Literature on December 10, 2001. It is a matter of pride for Naipaul to have been honored by the Swedish academy on the 100th anniversary of the institution of the Noble Prize. In 2008, *The Times* ranked Naipaul seventh on their list of '50 greatest British writers since 1945'. Moreover, he is an honorary doctorate from Cambridge University, London and Columbia University, New York. He expired on 11 August 2018, at the age of 85.

Critics hold different opinions about Naipaul's attitude to life. Naipaul's three collections of short stories are seen by critics as some of the finest expressions of the dilemmas and struggle of colonized people striving to make both their individual and social lives meaningful in a post-colonial context. Naipaul's fellow travel writer and friend, Paul Theroux, considers his collection of short stories as masterpieces in the fiction of rootlessness. While nearly all critics have praised the charming prose style and delicate humor of the stories, many commentators most often from the developing world, have charged that even in the early works, Naipaul paints pictures of the Third World people as culturally inferior. However, regardless of critics' comments, he is one of the most eminent writers all over the world, as his popularity and output testify it.

(b) Diasporic Writings: An Overview

Diaspora literature involves an idea of a homeland—a place from where the displacement occurs—and narratives of harsh journeys undertaken and an account of economic compulsions. Diaspora is a minority community living in exile or as expatriates. *The Oxford English Dictionary*, 1989, edition (second) traces the etymology of the word 'Diaspora' back to its Greek roots. *The Oxford English Dictionary* cites the major type of dispersal—the Jews living dispersed among the gentiles after the captivity. The word dispersal signifies the location of a fluid human autonomous space wherein people move in a complex set of nostalgia and desire for the homeland and the compulsion of making of a new home in the host nation.

The later edition of *The Oxford English Dictionary* refers the word 'Diaspora' as the movement of people from any nation or group away from their own country. So, the term 'Diaspora', originally used for dispersal from one's homeland is for all expatriates, refugees, exiles and immigrants, whose lives and experiences have been altered by paradigms of bilingualism, biculturalism and geographical dislocations.

The growing size of the diaspora has entailed features such as dislocation, disintegration, dispossession and disbelongingness. Manjit Inder Singh explains how these features define diasporic discourses: "The idea or the principle of understanding behind a body of diasporic 'discourse' primarily relates to the historical stages through which the populace of a country has undergone to economic, political, sociological, and military and other pressures or compulsions" (Singh 49).

Diasporic writers are deeply attached to their centrifugal homeland, yet yearn to belong to their current abode. They suffer double marginalization by the neglect at the hands of their root culture and when their host disproves their belonging to the receiving land. This condition of being 'unhomed' is associated further with alienation, a desire to reclaim the past yet revolt against it, the yearning to go back forestalled by the inability to move out, and the urge to show solidarity to the homeland but unwillingness to threaten relations with the host country.

The diasporic authors engage in cultural transmission that is equitably exchanged in the manner of translating a map of reality for multiple readerships. Besides, they are equipped with bundles of memories which are articulated as an amalgam of global and national strands that embody real and imagined experience. Salman Rushdie has also brought out the agony of being an expatriate.

Diasporas of the today's world are a result of the complicated process of the colonized societies interacting with the colonizing nations. For example, India, Africa, Canada and the West Indies have distinct diasporic backgrounds through which the respective writer's work produces varied issues.

Therefore, one can state that Diaspora is an emotional and psychological situation of the struggle between regression and progression, dislocation and then, relocation.

Diaspora relates to history and culture and the experience of inhabiting these two. History specific and culture specific spaces yield to a genuine tension of dislocation and alienation. The strategy to counter such a cultural shock of a migrant, as he tries to build multiple identities, is to develop a hybrid vision that at the end becomes an ongoing process for adaption. One comes across tremendous creativity, hetroglosia, hybridity (mostly positive) and linguistic experimental concerns (against 'othering') and gender subalternity; voice do come in most of the time and that is refreshing departure from the earlier more or less monolithic Anglo-American-centric, or Euro-centric one which one worked with a few decades back.

India has a history of diasporic groups. There are so many prominent Diasporic writers from India. Some of them are Anita Desai, Amitav Ghosh, Bharati Mukherjee, Salman Rushdie, Vikram Seth, Chitra Banerjee Divakaruni and Shashi Tharoor.

Anita Desai was born on June 24, 1937, in Mussoorie, India. Since she grew up in India and did most of her writings here, one may wonder at her inclusion among diasporic writers of India. Her two novels deal brilliantly with the difficult situation of immigrants: Indians in Britain in *Bye-Bye Blackbird* (1971) and Germans in India in *Baumgartner's Bombay* (1988). She has said in an interview that she looks India with a "Certain detachment", that "certainly comes from [her] mother", "I feel about India as on Indian, But I suppose I think about it's an outside" (Desai 522). *Bye-Bye Blackbird* largely focuses on the theme of immigration and alienation. It is set in London and deals with the problems faced by Indian immigrants. It juxtaposes two friends, Adit Sen, a well settled and culturally assimilated person, who still thinks himself alienated and finally goes back to India and his friend Dev, who encounters flagrant racial prejudices, though still he decides to stay on. However, Adit's feeling of alienation in Britain leads him to India.

Baumgartner's Bombay, Anita Desai's masterpiece, is written from the outsiders' perspective, and in which the protagonist is an immigrant who is alienated from the society. He comes to India just before World War II to seek refugee but ironically meets his fate while spending fifty years in India, he is killed by a drug addict. The protagonist of *Baumgartner's Bombay* is a German refugee in India. Desai's long-time desire to include the German part of her heritage in her work must have prompted her to write a novel about a German in Bombay. Shirley Chew remarks that it was "inevitable" and Anita Desai has brought together the two strands of her heritage, Indian and German.

Another Diasporic writer named Leena Dhingra was born in India. She left her native country in her childhood. After the partition of India and Pakistan in 1947, her home which was in Pakistani part, was lost to her and her family became uprooted. During her school days, she moved between India, France, England and Europe. Dhingra's works mostly emphasize on the theme of cultural displacement, isolation and exile. In her narratives, different cultures come together but disintegrated which leads to a sense of fragmentation. Moreover, this loss and fragmentation is not only Dhingra's personal matter. It is a collective loss of family also who lost their home and city. This disintegration creates a psychic condition of rootlessness—what she calls an "identity of no identity". The feeling of a refugee is always present in her mind. She writes about this feeling: "The three pillars of my identity: of being Indian, free and a refugee" (Dhingra 104). The topic of Dhingra's another work "The Girl who could not See Herself" is the establishment of a valid identity. About which Dhingra writes: "Once upon a time there was a girl who couldn't see herself very clearly, and so she kept stumbling and losing herself all the time. For since she couldn't see herself, she didn't know what she was, or where she fitted in, or how she should behave" (Dhingra 1). The girl in the story could not see herself. She gets only a hazy image of herself while looking in the mirror, so she decides to ask others about herself. One day when a man tells her that she has a beautiful smile only then she is able to see her whole-self in the mirror. Thus, the identity of a girl, then, is established through the positive response of the man. This process could be considered as a metaphor for the situation of the immigrant woman who makes great efforts to achieve her identity which is not possible without a positive response from the environment. Dhingra's first novel, *Amritvela* is about the homecoming of young Indian woman named Meera, who was taken to England and is brought up there by her parents. Meera is married to an Englishman and has a young daughter. When her husband gets a promotion and moves to another town, they live separately. She feels isolated in England so she decides to go to India with her daughter to start a new life there. The novel depicts her experiences in India, and the discovery of her roots in the cultural heritage and then her final return to England. At the beginning of the novel *Amritvela*, Meera expresses her feelings in such a way: "I feel myself to be suspended between two cultures, then this is where I belong, the half way mark. Here in the middle of nowhere, up in the atmosphere, is my space—the half-way point between East and West" (Dhingra 29.) Thus, it is the feeling of cultural displacement that makes her desirous to look for her roots in India. According to Pratap Chatterjee, *Amritvela* draws on the autobiographical elements of Dhingra.

Amitav Ghosh has also a personal as well as professional interest in diasporas. He was born in 1956 in Calcutta but was raised in Bangladesh, Sri Lanka, and Iran. The common themes of Ghosh's fiction are emigration, exile and cultural displacement while travelling across continents and culture is a major subject of Ghosh's first novel, *The Circle of Reason*. This novel is a serious attempt to deal with man's delusive quest that has taken many Third World workers and professionals across the world in search of a better life. It is a story of a boy and his adventure in three different parts of the world:

rural Bengal, the Middle Eastern City of at Al-Ghazira and El-Oued, a desert town in Algeria. The first part of the book has a number of incidental observations on Indian migration. Ghosh also provides details about a large number of migrants but in the central part of the novel one gets to see Ghosh's diasporic consciousness and the insecure lives lived by migrant workers. At the end of the novel, the major characters resume their travel again, in the backdrop of migrating birds filling the sky as they move and make their annual flights between Europe and Africa.

Ghosh's *The Shadow Lines* continues the writer's increasing interest in his theme of immigrant life and the diasporic consciousness, though the novel does not directly depict Indian diaspora. The first section of the novel indicates how a chain of events can be set in motion by an overseas trip. The mass migration of Bengalis to England is one aspect of the Indian Diaspora depicted in the narrative. In 1939, thirteen years before the narrator's birth, his father's aunt, Mayadebi, had left for England with her husband and eight years old son. So, the novel offers a glimpse into the lives of these migrants.

Bharati Mukherjee, a prominent writer among the writers of Indian diaspora, was born in Calcutta. She contributed a lot to the diasporic literature by writing novels, short stories, non-fictional prose, socio-political commentaries, journal articles and interview. Her *The Tiger's Daughter* is the story of a 22 years old girl, Tara Banerjee, who is married to an American writer, David. She revisits India after a seven years' stay in the U.S. In this way, *The Tiger's Daughter* is read as nostalgic journey "back" home. Mukherjee's another work, *Wife,* is a story of a girl named Dimple Dasgupta, who marries Amit Basu, a consulting engineer and is about to emigrate to the U.S. On account of her sudden transportation from Calcutta to New York, she goes into a shock and becomes unable to cope with the trauma of leaving home. Her husband is unable to understand her anguish and terror in such a dislocation and calls it a 'cultural shock'. Slowly, she starts with a few meaningless acts of cruelty and finally, kills her husband with a kitchen knife, which shows an ultimate gesture of fragmentation and despair.

Mukherjee's *Darkness*, a collection of concise description of immigrant experiences, is dedicated to her son Malamud, the stories which do justice to both Mukherjee and Malamud. In the introduction to *Darkness*, she states about psychological and emotional energy that motors all immigrants. She writes: "For a writer, energy is aggression; urgency colliding with confidence" (Mukherjee 10).

Another writer of Indian Diaspora is V.S. Naipaul who was born in 1932 in Chaguanas, on the island of Trinidad. Chaguanas was an Indian village recreated by indentured laborers. Naipaul's grandfather had come to Trinidad as an indentured laborer and stayed on. Naipaul, from his first non-fiction on India *An Area of Darkness* (1964), had begun his painful confrontation with the civilization that had nurtured him in his formative years, to which he become alien.

India: A Wounded Civilization, Naipaul's second book on India, agitated many Indians and liberal friends. Naipaul was furious with India for not shaping up well after the independence. However, by 1990s Naipaul had changed his views about India, especially in the book *India: A Million Mutinies Now*. This book is a splendid work of different changes and developments in India.

Thus, Naipaul's all three books on India, *An Area of Darkness, India: A Wounded Civilization* and *India: A Million Mutinies Now* represent three different yet related stages of his life-long struggles with himself and search for identity.

Meena Alexander, another Indian writer in Diaspora, was born on February 17, 1951, in Allahabad, India. Her father was an employee of the Indian Government and was sent to North Africa when Alexander was five, and as result, she would spent six months at a time on each continent, but her identity remained anchored in India. After finishing her doctoral thesis, she returned to India, where, she lectured in English at various Indian universities including, Delhi University, JNU, and the University of Hyderabad from 1974 to 1979. Within two years after she returned to India, her first poetic volume, *The Bird's Bright Ring*, was published. In 1979, she left India for New York, which filled her with a sense of displacement and loss. Fortunately, that loss was compensated when Alexander realized that her involvement into the uncontrolled pulse of New York City could intensify her creative imagination. She opines about this possibility: "[New York] is a world of people like me. All shapes and substances here.... It is a great city, with an enormous energy of life. And that attracts me as an Indian, because I also come from a place teeming with life" (Alexander 25).

Alexander's feminism and the diasporic consciousness that characterize much of her writings are deeply rooted in India and in her childhood days when she used to travel back and forth continents. Diasporic consciousness is evident in several of Alexander's poems but it is a prominent feature of *Nampally Road*, a short novel set entirely in India. This novel is based on Alexander's own experiences. The story is told by Mira Kannadical, an English instructor at a local college, who has returned to Hyderabad, India, after studying in England. The novel records Mira's attempt to understand the various changes in her homeland as she views the extremely unhelpful consequences of civil unrest. Mira struggles hard to define herself and her heritage: "As for the Indian past, what was it to me? Sometimes I felt it was a motley collection of events that rose in the abandoned graveyard the boy picked his way through. I had no clear picture of what unified it all, what our history might. We were in it, all together, that's all I knew. And there was no way out" (Alexander 28).

Alexander continues her exploration of diasporic themes in her autobiography, *Fault Lines*, and in various volumes of short poems, which bring together the two aspects of her life—that of rural Kerala in India, and that of Manhattan: confused and crowded.

Kamala Markandaya, another writer of Indian Diaspora, born in 1924 in India, is a south Indian Brahmin from an upper middle-class background. Her father worked for the railways and used to travel far and wide. So her keen observation during the travels increased her interest in creative writing. She married an English man in 1948, and has been living in England and writing novels ever since. Her novels deal with both Indian and British characters and have the clash of Eastern and Western values and customs. Her novels depict hardships and integrity of the women characters. Her first novel, *Nectar in a Sieve* has been translated into seventeen languages. It explores the threatening effects of English industrialism that strongly changed the lifestyle of Indian villagers. Another novel by her, *Possession*, set in England and Indian background, raises an issue of ownership. In this novel, a swami encourages a shepherd boy named Valmiki, who paints Hindu gods and goddesses on rock. Caroline Bell takes him to England and he becomes famous overnight. Though he is pleased with his fame, he cannot give up his values and traditions, like for instance, his strict vegetarianism. But Caroline's influence changes him completely and he does not even go to see his dying mother. Valmiki soon realizes his native pull and has to return to his roots. Caroline produces fake letters and tries to spoil his love relationship with another woman so that she can continue her relation with Valmiki but he breaks off all his ties with Caroline and returns to his caves with the help of Anasuya. Thus, it is a novel dealing with the psychological issues of ownership in relationship and the theme of cultural alienation.

Shashi Tharoor, a well-known name among Indian Diasporas, was born in England on 9 March 1956. He did his schooling in Bombay and Calcutta and graduated from Delhi. He started working at United Nations in 1978, and has worked with refugee settlement and peacekeeping activities. His *The Great Indian Novel* is a significant work of literature. It retells the history of contemporary India like Salman Rushdie's *Midnight's Children* and uses the major incidents of the last nine decades. He retells the *Mahabharata* itself as a political allegory and uses the ancient epic device of a non-participating narrator. Through this novel, Tharoor satirizes India and the cause of Indian political anarchy.

Tharoor's another masterpiece, *The Five Dollar Smile and Other Stories*, is a collection of fourteen stories. The titular story comes from the poster pasted on billboards and bulletin boards across the world asking the people to donate charity that try to get smile on a child's face. The story brings forth the emotions of the recipient of charity who is represented in familiar posters. A twelve years old boy Joseph Kumaran, on a flight to the United States, remembers how he was shocked by a photographer while visiting an orphanage in India for a suitable subject. The photographer says: "Get him away from that food sister.... We want a hungry child, not a feeding one" (*FDS* 15).

Salman Rushdie, another illustrious Diasporic writer, is regarded as one of the most prestigious authors who inaugurated the field of postcolonial diasporism with his writings. He was born into an affluent Muslim family in Bombay on June 19, 1947. In 1967, his parents moved to Pakistan and he started visiting Pakistan because of his family's migration to Karachi from Bombay. Rushdie notes about his multiple affiliations: "Three places have more or less an equal claim on me.... England where I live, India...where I was born, Pakistan where my family lives" (Kaufman 22). Each of these places can be legitimately a subject of his writings. Rushdie wrote a series of essays, where he reflected his location as an 'author from three countries' and as an expatriate writer pointing to the gain and losses, as it were between two or more cultures.

Rushdie's debut novel, *Grimus*, was an attempt to show the difficult situation of alienation. The story follows Flapping Eagle, a young Indian who receives the gift of immortality after drinking a magic fluid. Flapping Eagle, an Axona Indian, is excluded from the society because of his fairer complexion. In search of his identity, Flapping is tired of the earthly reality of immorality and wants to get rid of the Grimus effect. Hence, the novel apparently demonstrates that migrants have no future, neither on Mortal Island nor on Immortal one. They could wander wherever they wish but without carrying their heart with them.

Rushdie's *Midnight's Children* paved the way for post-colonial literature in India. Like Salman Rushdie, the protagonist Saleem Sinai, wanders among three countries, i.e.

India, Pakistan and Bangladesh but unable to find a proper place to live in. In this narrative, he pictures the trauma of fluid identity. Here Saleem Sinai is presented as a miniature of all diasporic generations; how they are treated in the newly inhabited territories. Saleem being the mouthpiece of his creator expresses the feelings that Rushdie feels while living in an adopted land. Thus, *Midnight's Children* is a narrative of displacement and rootlessness that is caused by relocation. All Midnight's Children, Saleem, Shiva, Padma and Parvati face a calamity of identity, disintegration of disposition and geographical as well as a cultural dislocation. Rushdie clarifies these impulses behind situations: "When the Indian who writes from outside India tries to reflect that world, he is obliged to deal in broken mirrors, some of whose fragments have been irretrievably lost" (Rushdie 11).

Cultural displacement has forced the immigrant writers to accept the provisional nature of all truths and certainties. It is almost impossible for migrants to be unable to call to mind their native place and nativity emotionally. Consequently, this displacement constitutes a double identity that is at once singular, plural and partial. In *Imaginary Homelands*, Rushdie echoes this notion: "Our identity is at once plural and partial. Sometimes we feel that we straddle two cultures, at other time we fall between two cultures, at other time we fall between two stools. But however, ambiguous and shifting this ground may be it is not an infertile territory for a writer to occupy" (Rushdie 15).

Shame, the most popular political adventure of Rushdie, exhibits the trauma of migration that he has been facing throughout his life. It is a novel about migration and at several places Salman Rushdie emerges as the narrator and narrates the miserable conditions of migrants in line with what he confesses in one of his interviews with Ashutosh Varshney:

> It is a novel about the changes that happen to individuals and communities under the pressure of migration.... I wanted to talk about the immigrant community in London particularly the South Asian community, and at that time

> what I wanted to say about it is, "Here's this enormous community of people who are, it seems, invisible—their concerns their lives you know, their fears and so on, somehow invisible to the white population" (Rushdie 19).

Like all migrants, Salman Rushdie has not been able to shake off the idea of roots and identity. These roots help the migrants in his novels to be in touch of his nativity. The theme of root, route and rootlessness has become an explicit part of Rushdie's plot. His novels describe the psychological crisis resulting from the loss of identity and roots and this happens to almost each and every diasporic and post-colonial author. Rushdie depicts the actual position of migrants—what they get and what they lose: "When individual comes unstuck from their native land, they are called migrants. When nations do the same thing (Bangladesh), the act is called succession. I may be such a person. Pakistan may be such a country" (Rushdie 86).

Rushdie describes his own position further in these words: "I am an emigrant from one country (India) and a new comer in two (England), where I live and Pakistan to which my family moved against my will" (Rushdie 85).

As an immigrant, who move from one place to another, region to region, Rushdie's identity becomes hybrid and fluid because of these geo-cultural movements. The migrant may live in new places but that is only as imaginary homeland—he never feels comfort in their newly occupied home or country.

Moyez G. Vassanji, another writer of the Indian diaspora, was born on 30 May, 1950. He is a Canadian novelist and editor whose works have been acknowledged universally and known throughout North America, Africa, and South Asia, and later have been translated into several languages. Vassanji's writings deal with the issues of migration, diaspora, citizenship, gender and ethnicity and have received substantial critical applause from academic circles. Vassanji is a diasporic writer and what makes his work apart from other Canadian writers is his minute depiction of the multiple migrations of his South Asian characters.

Vassanji's first novel *The Gunny Sack* (1989) is the story of Indian community in East Africa. It is a narrative about four generations of Asians in Tanzania with the themes of identity, displacement and race relations worked out at several levels—personal, familial, social and political. It also has autobiographical traces. Huseni Salim Juma is the protagonist who is also known as Kala. He experiences a journey down the reminiscences through the heirloom left behind by his grand aunt, Ji Bai. This bequest is in the form of a gunny sack which is a compelling emblem of recollection in the novel. The novel displays complex interrelationships of the characters and events that compete for attention as the cluttered object in Ji Bai's gunny sack prompts an overflow of remembrances of equally fragmented experiences.

The novel connects the remote past with the present through the flash-back technique and undeviating narration. Kala explores and finds his origins and in the process that unfolds his family background bit by bit. Vassanji registers the complex social structure with imperial centers of power, the colonial powers—the German, the English and the Portuguese—who fight with each other to exploit and enslave the natives. *The Gunny Sack,* was awarded a Commonwealth Literature Regional First Nobel prize in 1990 and later published in a German translation.

Vassanji's second novel, *No New Land* (1991), is set in Canada in the mid-70s and is about an Asian family who migrated from Africa to Toronto, Canada. The novel is situated in Toronto, and represents a group of Indians from Tanzania which is trying to adapt to life in a new land. The novel humorously and tragically illustrates how the past always chases the present and the future. The story is all about Nurdin Lalani and his family who are Asian immigrants from Africa and have come to the Toronto suburb of Don Mills only to find as the old world and its beliefs, still follow them. Nurdin Lalani, a genial orderly at a downtown hospital, has been a suspect of sexually assaulting a girl. Though he is guiltless, his customary modesty prompts him to doubt the chastity of his own thoughts. Eventually, his friendship with the liberal

Sushila offers him appealing freedom from the past that haunts him and a marriage that has become a routine with the trials of coping with teenage children.

However, the title of the novel proposes that the land where Nurdin and his friends have moved is not a new land, but it has undergone many other been a site of many waves of migrations—first, the English and the French then the Portuguese and at last the Italians and the Africans. *No New Land* is a very well-written text that familiarizes the readers with brilliantly drawn characters who are trapped between the two worlds. Vassanji then observes how the survivals of these characters are perturbed by their relocations.

Vassanji's third novel, *The Book of Secrets,* was published in 1994 and is an intricate account of the fictionalized Shamsi Muslim community in East Africa. In 1988, a retired school teacher named Pius Femandes finds an old diary in the back room of an East African shop which was written in 1913 by a British colonial administrator. The diary arouses the curiosity of Femandes, whose fascination with the stories it contains gradually connects the past with present and reveals the story of banned liaisons, family secrets and cultural exiles that leads him on fact-finding journey through his past and Africa's past.

Vassanji's next novel, *Amriika* (1999), is set in America. This novel is all about betrayal, disillusionment and discovery. The story documents the experiences of an immigrant named Ramji who is a middle-aged Shamsi of Indian origin and comes to America in 1968 to study at a technological institute in America and his struggle at negotiating identity in a new land stands in total contrast to the values that he has carried all along as baggage from his homeland. Later, he also becomes an eyewitness to anti-Vietnam war demonstrations, peace marches, and the growth of religious cults, fast-changing sexual mores and values. As far as his personal life is concerned, he has bittersweet experiences in marriage, adulterous relationships and children, as he goes on with his search for a meaningful and authentic life.

Ramji finds himself pulled by the riotous current of those troubled times; he sweeps up in events whose consequences will haunt him for years to come. He becomes displaced in the hub of immigrant vicious forces. Thus, *Amriika*, maps the fate of a realm during three important phases as it foregrounds the theme of rootlessness on the individual level. Ramji finds himself drawn into such a setting, which grasps frightening recaps of the past and its unreciprocated queries. The novel is a story where the protagonist tries to bridge the gap between dream and reality, but fails and becomes a wanderer.

Nirad C. Chaudhuri, one more distinguished figure in the area of diaspora literature, was born on 23rd November 1897 in East Bengal, British India (now Bangladesh). He was the second of eight children of Upendra Narayan Chaudhuri who was a lawyer. His mother was Sushila Sundarani Chaudhurani. His parents were liberal middle-class Hindus. His family shifted to Calcutta in 1910 where he got his primary education at home and then continued to study in a small town primary school. He completed his graduation from Calcutta University where he secured the first rank in his BA (Honours) examination in History. He had a long period of being unemployed. From 1921 to 1941, he remained in Calcutta and started to work as a literary journalist who used to write columns in newspapers, both in English and Bengali. In 1992, he moved to Delhi, where he was offered a position in All India Radio and worked as a Broadcaster. In 1947 he started to work on his first book, *The Autobiography of an Unknown Indian* and got it published in 1951 in England. It can be read on many levels and it is very much a story of Chaudhuri's life till his twenty-fifth year but written from the perspective of a fifty-year-old man. It is also a record of the people who live in small towns and rural Bengal. Chaudhuri also presents the lovable portrayals of his parents who had shaped his life.

The central chapter of *The Autobiography of an Unknown Indian* titled "Torch Race of the Indian Renaissance", praises the hybrid culture of that was formed when English culture refreshed the Bengali mind in the nineteenth century. While *The Autobiography of an Unknown Indian*, is a celebration of the Bengali Renaissance, it is also a lament for a period that has passed away. He states in this connection, "all that we have learnt, all that we have acquired, and all that we have prized is threatened with extinction" (Chaudhuri 127). He felt assimilated with the cultural life that he had experienced in Kishoreganj as a child but when he was fourteen he came to Calcutta and with his arrival he began to have a feeling of alienation from his social group and he writes in despair, "once torn up from my natural habitat I became liberated from the habitat altogether; my environment and I began to fall apart, and in the end the environment became wholly external" (Chaudhuri 257-58). And this is where his diasporic consciousness began to proclaim in him for the very first time and would lead him further to choose exile away from Bengal. This book made Chaudhuri famous and he had got an invitation to visit Britain in 1955 by the British Broadcasting Corporation. *A Passage to England* was his second major publication and published in 1959. His third book, *The Continent of Circe, Being an Essay on the Peoples of India* (1965) holds a very highly quirky view of Indian history and civilization. This book won him the Duff Memorial Prize in 1967. He retired from his job in 1952 but continued to write in Delhi. During this period, he has written two books named *The Intellectual in India* (1967) and *To Live or Not to Live*! (1970). These works are published in India and offer guidance to Indians on how to live happily in their own country. Through the first three books, the reputation he has made in West, led to an invitation from the family members of the famous Indologist Max Muller to write a biography of him and he had to move to Oxford in 1970. After finishing this work, he was asked to write a biography of Robert Clive, who was the founder of the British Empire in India. This got published in 1975 as *Clive of India*. His other commissioned work, *Hinduism; A Religion to Live By* (1979), shows his keen interest in the subject, religion. By the end of the seventies, he was running short of funds and was about to return back to India but soon got an opportunity to write a sequel to his book, *The Autobiography of an Unknown Indian*, and got it published in 1987 as *Thy*

Hand, Great Anarch! India, 1921–1952. At the time of writing Autobiography, Chaudhuri was witnessing the destruction of Bengal as being a part of the large process; it was a part of the degradation of the whole country itself. This was the major theme of and the central idea of *Thy Hand, Great Anarch!* It is also a theme of *The Continent of Circe* as he marked it the cultural suicide of India and a "Phase of unrelieved decay" (Chaudhuri 127) by diminishing the realm and the philosophy it had formed. He was also awarded honorary D. Phil from the University of Oxford in 1990. Chaudhuri was a prolific writer and continued to live in exile in England, severing all his connections with his homeland. Even in the last years of his life, this leading figure of the Indian diaspora, published his last work at the age of 99. His wife Amiya Chaudhuri died in 1994 in Oxford, England. He too died at Oxford in 1999, three months before completing his 102nd birthday.

David Dabydeen is another writer of Indian Diaspora, who was born on a sugar plantation in Guyana, in December 1955. At the age of twelve, he migrated to England and was reared up by local authorities as his parents were divorced. He studied English in Cambridge and London Universities and attained his doctorate degree in 1982. Dabydeen, being a man of South Asian origin, was ashamed of his food, foreign dress and language which were regarded as an indication of inferiority. He was sensitized by racial isolation and inferiority at his early age that was later marked by racial violence in Guyana. Dabydeen has decided to dedicate his scholarly life to working with black scholars to bring black people to the center and to give them the power of speech. He asserts that, "any scholarship relating to black people should not be divorced from consideration of contemporary racist realities, and should not be separated from the struggles to combat such racism" (*Hogarth's Blacks* viii).

In his first edited book, *Hogarth's Blacks: Images of Blacks in Eighteenth Century English Art* (1987), Dabydeen, has reread Hogarth's dramatic narrative, an eighteenth-century painter who brings the black people into his pictures and the twentieth-century scholar who brings them to center. According to Dabydeen, Hogarth's objective was to use blacks to mock the English upper class. At the same time, Hogarth also aligns blacks with the other victims of commercialism and colonialism who had sometimes participated in the rituals of English peasantry. He further states, if Hogarth's mocking objectives are missed, the painter "can be deemed to have reflected or reinforced racism among his white contemporaries" (*Hogarth's Blacks* 113). David Dabydeen's *Hogarth, Walpole and Commercial Britain* (1985) which is an extension of *Hogarth's Blacks*, examines Hogarth's moralistic message that covers a deeper political intention and discloses his intentions to castigate the government.

Dabydeen's first collection of poems, *Slave Song* (1984) is the winner of the Commonwealth Poetry Prize 1984, and the Quiller-Couch Prize at Cambridge. *Slave Song* is "largely concerned with an exploration of the erotic energies of the colonial experience, ranging from a corrosive to a lyrical sexuality" ("Introduction to *Slave Song*" 34). *Slave Song* exposes the heart-rending realities of Guyanese history and Dabydeen feels sorry for wasted lives, broken bodies, weakened minds where readers pain for people's distress, at points in the collection.

Dabydeen's *Coolie Odyssey*, is the second book of poems, published in 1988, which recaptures the movement of indentured laborers from India to Guyana and later relates the diaspora of Guyanese to England. Life in Guyana is existed in grime, between the ideal territory of memory (India), and the awe-inspiring worlds like England and North America. Like all West Indians, the Indo-Guyanese is also troubled by disintegration and rootlessness. In *Coolie Odyssey*, Dabydeen once again, returns to the demoralizing outcomes of racial ferocity in Guyana.

Dabydeen's next novel named *The Intended* is an autobiographical novel that was published in 1991. Here narrator recollects his early years that he had spent in the villages of Guyana. It later follows the flight from Guyana to England, where the West Indian remains an immigrant, where old desires are compounded by new longings and old homelessness by new rootlessness and alienation.

In England, the narrator is overwhelmed by a deep sense of shame whether it is language, food, dressing, all are the reasons for humiliation and self-loathing. Once again, Dabydeen remembers the racial division between Indo- and Afro-Guyanese as depicted in *Slave Song* and *Coolie Odyssey*. This is agonizingly when one of the narrator's friends Nasim is chased by a gang of white people into the path of a car and is injured severely. In the hospital, he "looked small and lost, like pictures of hungry Third World children we saw on television" (*The Intended* 14). The narrator responds shamefully and angrily at the victim and asserts, "I hated him. A strange desire to hurt him, to kick him, overcame me" (*The Intended* 14). This hatred of wounded self and others finds expression in his deep desire for acceptance through his works.

One more writer of the Indian diaspora is Sujata Bhatt. She was born on May 5, 1956, in Ahmedabad. She was born in India but her parents moved to the United States when she was twelve. Bhatt is bicultural as she was born and brought up in India but spent her adolescence and early adulthood in the United States and tri-cultural by marriage as she married a German Writer named Michael Augustin, who she met at the University of Iowa while working on M.F.A. She started writing poetry when she was eight years old. She was also a writer-in-residence at the University of Victoria, Canada for some time. At present, she lives in Germany and works as a freelance writer and translates Gujarati Poetry into English. She writes about the realities of day-to-day life of America, Europe and India, in her poetry. She recreates the ordinary subject of her South Asian childhood world like rich smells, tastes, textures, colors, in many of her poems, both in *Brunizem* (1988), her first published volume and in *Monkey Shadows* (1991), her second collection. The second work has writings on lizards, pregnant goats, water buffalos, leopards, cobras, elephants, funeral pyres, marigolds, cow dung, tulsi leaves, mango trees, warm chapattis, red chilies, and an exclusive taste of garlic, aromatic flavored ghee and henna and gives her readers access to the most ordinary subjects of this world. In one of her poems "Go to Ahmedabad" from her collection,

Brunizem, Bhatt presents her enduring love for her place and its people. Many of her poems deal with the memories of India, the anticipation of awakening sexuality and other short-lived moments whether pleasurable or not.

In her second volume, *Monkey Shadows,* as the title predicts, many poems are about monkeys. The first poem in this collection, "The Langur Coloured Night," evokes the delicate wildness of the animal's "cry" as voiced "truth". The second poem, "The Stare," stables "human child" and "monkey child" in a firm stare and affirms that each creature is too innocent to apprehend the sound between them. Like other animals, Elephants are also significant in this collection. "A Different Way to Dance" ends with a child's sad reflection on the story of Shiva, Parvati and their son Ganesh. Who is an Elephant headed God, who was born with a normal head. His father Shiva, in heat of the moment, beheaded his own son Ganesh and then in regret cut an Elephant's head and offered the Elephant's head to Ganesh. The speaker cannot get rid of thinking about the headless elephant and the subsequent poem, "What Happened to the Elephant," continues the contemplation. Most of Bhatt's poems deal with the subjects like female experiences, including sexuality, and she holds an opinion about the equality of men and women and believes that both should be given equal opportunities and options to grow in life. Though she writes in English, Bhatt's first language is Gujarati; she uses Gujarati in her poems to celebrate her racial legacy. She cherishes both her Indian family beliefs and her American confidence but feels homeless living in Germany as she is not fully confident in the language and she does not appreciate the atmosphere of the country and feels suffocated, though she pays her rare visits to England and Holland and enjoys the same. Bhatt's poetry collections have received international praise from reviewers and she has been awarded a number of poetry prizes in the United Kingdom including a Cholmondeley Award (1991), the Commonwealth Poetry Prize for Asia (1989), and the Alice Hunt Bartlett Prize (1988). She has also been chosen as a receiver of the Poetry Book Society Recommendation for *Monkey Shadows*. Further, Bhatt's public readings of her works have also got tremendous appreciation with similar delight and this is why she can be counted as one of the important writers of the Indian diaspora.

Another writer of Indian diasporic named, Agha Shahid Ali was born in Delhi and grew up in Kashmir. Traveling between Delhi, Srinagar and Jammu, Ali came to the United States for the very first time in 1961 and lived there for three years. He has done his B.A. in English from the University of Kashmir in 1968 and M.A. in English in 1970 from the University of Delhi. In 1984, he received his Ph.D. in English from Pennsylvania State University. From 1970 to 1975, he worked as a lecturer and published his first book of poetry, *Bone-Sculpture* in 1972, which depicts a life that is committed to material corruption. Ali started writing from the age of ten and came across a strong sense of familial and cultural resources as he dealt with the theme of separation. His wrote his second book of poetry, *In Memory of Begum Akthar* (1979) when he was writing and studying in the United States, where Ali gives a glimpse of past to his audience that elucidates his concern with the issues like death, separation and loss. Ali's other notable work, *The Half-Inch Himalayas,* records his efforts to retrieve the past without being bound by it. This work accounts for the problems of exile and documents an important stage in the journey of a writer of the Indian diaspora. Through this work he recreates the past and provides his own version of it. The loss that he talks about in this work is a loss of local habitation, named Kashmir. The price of exile is estimated in loneliness and worry that becomes a theme of his several poems. His another poem "A Call" accounts the speaker's isolation and nervousness as well as his childlike fear that he will be displaced from the affections of his parents by the cold moon of Kashmir whereas in "Houses", he expresses just an opposite concern of a parent worrying about his absent child.

Ali's next collection of poems, *A Walk Through the Yellow Pages* depicts a world of failed connections and exhausted language, in short, the modern American wasteland. Categorized by arrivals and departures, crossings and re crossings, Ali's next book named *A Nostalgist's Map of America*, evidences the poet's deep-rooted diasporic consciousness as announced by the title itself. *A Nostalgist's Map of America,* knits into an integrated strand of stories from diverse historical, political and cultural contexts. It further can be seen as a successful act of translation, for which Ali is outstandingly known. He retells the stories of Laila and Majnoon in "From Another Desert" which is a classic example of cultural translation that evolves as the thematic volume of search for the beloved. His next poem "Snow on the Desert" is all about the assimilation of varied cultural materials and a perfect example of fruitful hybridization and becomes the source of great strength for the poet of the Indian diaspora.

Santha Rama Rau, another leading writer of the Indian diaspora, was born on January 24, 1923. She lived in India but was educated in England and the United States. Her father, Sir Bengal Rama Rau served as Indian ambassador to South Africa, Japan and the United States. Her mother was also the first daughter of a Kashmiri Brahmin family to attend college and became a famous name in the health care industry in India. English was a common mother tongue in their home as throughout the marriage of her parents, they spoke to each other in English only. Having her roots in both the East and West, she has made a notable contribution as a novelist, biographer, and dramatist but she is best known as a travel writer.

Because of her father's diplomatic assignment at the age of six, Rau moved to England along with her family members, and received her primary education in England. Later, her family shifted to South Africa, where her father served as an Indian High Commissioner. For the very first time, she had witnessed the injustice of colonialism, when she read signs written "Indians, natives, and dogs are not allowed" (*Home to India* 3). She then realized that her family could go to a public movie house only when her father used his diplomatic privilege on their behalf. After a few years, Rau came back to India with her mother and sister and started to live in Mumbai with her grandparents. She also states about the complex structure of a traditional Indian family and writes in this connection that, "the great, complex system of family and religion and customs that produced the old India still operated" (*Gifts of Passage* 3). After two years, she went to the U.S. for further education. At Wellesley, she enrolled and majored in English and during her summer break, she worked as a writer. She had a youthful experience in America that prompts her to write about the country as, "It was a strange time for me—half in love with America, with its driving energy, its earnestness, its kindness, and its extraordinary beauty, half deploring its ignorance of conditions in the rest of the world, its smug self-righteousness, and its assumption of privilege" (*Gifts of Passage* 27). Soon after, she realized that she wanted to be a writer and published her first best-selling book, *Home to India*, in 1945, a year after her graduation.

In 1947, Rau left for Japan to serve as hostess for her father, who was appointed as the first ambassador of free India to Japan. Later, she travelled to Asia, Northern China and newly liberated Indonesia and based on her travels, she published her second book, *East of Home*, in 1950. She got married in 1952 to her friend Faubion Bowers, who was an American. They continued to travel throughout Europe but returned to India in the following year for the birth of their son. In 1956, she published *Remember the House*, a novel set in India. Later, she travelled to Africa, Asia and to Russia for her magazine *Holiday*. Her three travel books, *This Is India* (1954), *View to the Southeast* (1957), and *My Russian Journey* (1959) were based on the articles she had written for *Holiday*. She also wrote varied articles for popular magazines such as the *Redbook, New York Times Magazine, Vogue, House and Garden* and *Housekeeping*. Her *Remember the House* and the autobiography *Gifts of Passage* largely addresses the themes of clashes between Western and customary Indian ideals. Being a Western-educated Asian, she sought to integrate the two strains of her background, one, the pragmatism of the West and the second, the traditionalism of India. Her book, *Home to India* opens with her grandmother's greeting and a question directed to a sixteen-year-old who has spent her ten years abroad. She records the experiences of her discussion with her grandmother, where her grandmother says: "My dear

Child, where in India will we find a husband tall enough for you?" (*Home to India* 1). After that most of the book details mention the cultural shock that she encounters in India. Her novel, *Remember the House*, depicts the dilemma of a Western educated protagonist named, Baba, who is preoccupied with personal concerns about whether she should marry the man of her grandmother's choice or seek out a Western idea of romantic love. On a visit to southern India, she pays attention to her recollection of grandmother's views on arrange marriage and at the end of the novel, she acknowledges the superficiality of the Western views of life and finds her grandmother's opinion authentic and consequently opts for an arranged marriage. Through the depictions of life in rural India and the dazzling upper-class Bombay of the last days of British rules, the novel also reveals the changes in the life of a nation. In her own life, Rau was prepared to accept the two parts of her background by becoming a typical expatriate—a travel writer.

Uma Parmeshawaran, another renowned writer of the Indian diaspora was born in Madras in 1941 but she was raised in Nagpur and Jabalpur. In 1963, she was awarded a full bright scholarship and travelled to the United States and studied American Literature at Indiana University. She was awarded her Ph.D. in 1972. Later, she joined the Department of English at the University of Winnipeg, where she continued to write and teach.

Uma Parmeshawaran is a scholar and a creative writer. Her teaching interests are Commonwealth Literature and Creative Writing. Her poems and short stories have published in several journals and magazines. She has also written numerous intellectual articles and has published three books of literary criticism, *A Study of Representative Indo-English Novelists*, *Cyclical Hope Cyclical Pain*, and *The Perforated Sheet: Essays on Salman Rushdie's Art*.

Uma's works are a reflection of the Indian diaspora in one sense, especially the experiences of South Asian Indians in Canada, and more precisely in Winnipeg, the city where she has lived since 1966. Her play, *Rootless But Green Are the*

Boulevard Trees, was first published in 1979 and reprinted in *The Door I Shut Behind Me* (1990). Her sequence of poems, *Trishanku* (1988), is set in Winnipeg. These three works explore the lives and experiences of Indian immigrants and their struggle with the painful tasks of adjusting and claiming their new land because she realizes, as an immigrant, she is intensely Canadian and most of the Canadians are immigrants. Yet at the same time, she writes about a delightful difference, that has its origin in the rich cultures and traditions of her homeland.

Uma's Eton Award-winning short story, *The Door I Shut Behind Me* briefs about the intergenerational immigrant and intertextual experiences. The story starts with Chander's departure from India who moves through a crisis in the communal lives of the Bhave family from *Rootless But Green Are the Boulevard Trees* and concludes in *Trishanku.* Savitri Bhave is adjourned from her city and is joined by her husband Sharad, in Canada. Sharad assures Savitri about their children's well-being as immigrants. However, parents may be placed between past or present, between homeland and alien land, but their children will be all set to acclaim Canada as their own land. They are free to wear Canadian clothes and can speak Canadian English without accents. For their children, India is not their home but just a place to explore. In *Rootless But Green Are the Boulevard Trees,* Jayant, a young man ridicules Sharad Bhave's thought that one day Canada will give his children an environment full of self-respect and mysticism but *Trishanku* denotes that Jayant was wrong and Sharad was right. Uma's two major works, *Rootless But Green Are the Boulevard Trees* and *Trishanku* share the same themes. The former focuses on single-family whereas the latter explores an entire immigrant community and discovers its changing experiences and reactions and various phases of adaptation to a new homeland. *Rootless But Green Are the Boulevard Trees'* main focus is on the younger generation. It is about Bhave's children and their struggles in the form of interracial relationships, especially between males and females, the cruel reality of racism, feeling of alienation and a dilemma between the mainstream culture and parents. As it portrays the dilemma of the younger generation, one of the adults, Veejala Moghe, who is fed up with low academics and prejudices of the Canadian Universities, decides to return to India in the hope to get respect. In this connection, Uma Parmeshwaram raises the consciousness of Canadians where she intends to tell them that immigrants come empty-handed from their countries, though bring intellect, learning and knowledge with them.

In *Trishanku*, Uma adds a number of characters and builds a representative East Indian-Canadian community, that includes immigrants of all ages and sexes, of different time periods in Canada, from different vocations, different backgrounds and cultures in the homeland. This is how Uma Parmeshwaram has made community her protagonist by developing the character of the community more than an individual character. In fact, through *Trishanku*, she expresses clearly the individual memories, experiences and longings. Uma does not restrict individuality; rather she put individualism in the form of strong communal experiences. Her work *Trishanku* is a series of monologues, spoken by different characters and all these characters get meanings from each other. This range of experiences in the collection of different voices proposes the interdependence of individual and community. As a result, Uma ends the silence and isolation of immigrant people by giving them a place and voice in Canadian literature.

One more writer of the Indian diaspora, Zulfikar Ghose, was born on March 13, 1935, in Sialkot, which is now a part of West Pakistan after the partition of India. He spent his first seven years in the town with his extended rural family which was so untouched by any development and its people were so crude and rural. Ghose shifted to Bombay with his family members in 1942. For him, Bombay was largely a vast, Hindu metropolitan city. Living in this city was like inculcating in him a sense of belonging at the same time being a Muslim among Hindus infused in him the sense of an outsider. So in the last ten years of British rule in the country, he had grown up witnessing increasing enmity between these two religions. Observing the communal violence preceding the partition, Ghose comments that "lorries, collecting dead bodies, would pass by streets as though they were collecting garbage cans" (*Confessions* 31).

In 1952, Ghose left Bombay for England and it was a dual exile for him as it was a dilemma of leaving from a land in which he was an outsider and evolving to one in which he was a stranger. Spending his next seventeen years from 1952 to 1969 in England, he did his schooling from Sloane School, Chelsea, and graduated from the University of Keele in 1959. During his college days, he edited an anthology called *Universities' Poetry*. He also worked as a reporter for the *Observer* and wrote reviews for the *Western Daily Press*, the *Guardian*, and the *Times Literary Supplement*. From 1964 to 1969, he worked as a teacher and during his teaching days he collaborated on a book with one of his closest friends and a British writer named B.S. Johnson. They had also worked together on a book of short stories titled *Statement against Corpses*. He later, brought out two collections of poems, *The Loss of India* (1964) and *Jets from Orange* (1967), and two novels, *The Contradictions* (1966) and *The Murder of Azim Khan* (1967).

In 1969, Ghose relocated to Texas to take up a new teaching assignment at the University of Texas and lived for more than two decades in Austin, Texas. During these years, he had published eight novels, two critical works, and two volumes of poetry, quite a few essays, short stories and poems. In one of his essays entitled "Going Home" which was published in the *Toronto South Asian Review*, Ghose expresses his excitement of visiting his birthplace, Pakistan, after twenty-eight years. Ghose has often been described as a Pakistani writer by critics but if one remembers that the city in which Ghose was born, was then a part of India. Also, the city Bombay in which he grew up is a part of the country, where he was born. In the same essay, he speaks of his unending pursuit and states that "there are moments in our lives when we can hear the soul whisper its contentment that the long torment of being has been stilled as last" ("Going Home" 15).

In some respects, Ghose's early works especially the collection of poems entitled *The Loss of India*, the collection of short stories, written in collaboration with his friend B.S. Johnson named *Statement against Corpses* and two novels named *The Contradictions* and *The Murder of Aziz Khan* can be easily recognized as Indo-Pakistani writings as they represent the issues of history, colonialism, identity. They also enable the author to explore the experience of exile against a confirmable locale.

Ghose's next work, *Crump's Terms* explore the lives of Crump, a disillusioned and lonely teacher in London and his ex-wife Frieda. Both Crump and Frieda are marginalized figures. Crump craves to bring order in his classroom and in his life and the latter leaves Germany to avoid maltreatment, seeking to alleviate the dejection of homelessness. In his next collection of poems, *The Violent West* (1972) and his next novel, *Hulme's Investigations into Bogart Script* (1981), he moves to another phase that is less engrossed with form and more with language. The concern of language and its complex relation to reality becomes the justification for both the novel and his critical work *Hamlet, Prufrock and Language.* His three novels, *A New History of Torments* (1982), *Don Bueno* (1983) and *Figures of Enchantment* (1986) are set in Latin America. Regardless of the representation of characters who have no connection to India or Pakistan, the novels are almost not subjective and explore the issues of power, guilt, nation and history. During the last few years, there has been a significant interest in the works of Ghose and there have been several articles written by distinguished critics that evaluate the significance of Ghose's work that has helped to establish him as a chief postcolonial and contemporary writer of the Indian diaspora.

WORKS CITED

Alexander, Meena. *Nampally Road.* Mercury House, 1991.

Alexander, Meena. *The Bird's Bright Ring*, Writer's Workshop, 1976.

Bhatt, Sujata. *Brunizem.* Carcanet, 1988.

Bhatt, Sujata. *Monkey Shadows.* Carcanet, 1991.

Chaudhari, Nirad C. *A Passage to England.* St. Martin's Press, 1959.

Chaudhari, Nirad C. *The Autobiography of an Unknown India,* 1951; Reading Mass, 1989.

Chaudhari, Nirad C. *The Continent of Circe, Being an Essay on the Peoples of India.* 1965; rpt. Oxford University Press, 1967.

Chaudhari, Nirad C. *To Live or Not to Live! An Essay on Living Happily with Others.* Hind Pocket Books, 1970.

Chaudhari, Nirad C. *The Intellectual in India.* Vir Publishing House, 1967.

Dabydeen, David. *Hogarth's Blacks: Images of Blacks in Eighteenth Century English Art.* University of Georgia Press, 1987.

Dabydeen, David. *Slave Song.* Dungaroo Press, 1984.

Dabydeen, David. *The Black Presence in English Literature (Ed.).* Manchester University Press, 1985.

Dabydeen, David. *The Intended.* Secker and Warburg, 1991.

Dabydeen, David. "Introduction to Slave Song." *Literary Review.* 1990, 32-38.

Demas Bliss, Corinne. "Against the Current: A Conversation with Anita Desai." *Massachusetts Review.* 29: 3, 1988.

Dhingra, Leena, "The Girl who couldn't See Herself", *Right of Way* (ed.). Asian Women's Writers' Workshop, Women's Press, 1988. pp. 101-03.

Dhingra, Leena. *Amritvela.* Women's Press, 1988.

Dhingra, Leena. "Breaking Out of the Labels", *Watchers and Seekers: Creative Writings by Black Women in Britain* (ed.) Rhonda Cobham and Merle Collins, Women's Press, 1987. pp. 102-06.

Ghose, Zulfikar. *Confessions of a Native-Alien.* Routledge & Kegan Paul, 1965.

Ghose, Zulfikar. *The Contradictions.* Macmillan, 1966.

Ghose, Zulfikar. *The Loss of India.* Routledge & Kegan Paul, 1964.

Ghose, Zulfikar. *The Murder of Aziz Khan.* Macmillan, 1967.

Ghose, Zulfikar. *The Violent West.* Macmillan, 1972.

Hammer, Robert D. (ed.). *Critical Perspectives on V.S. Naipaul.* Heinemann Educational Books, 1979.

Herwitz, Daniel and Ashutosh Varshrey, *Midnight's Diaspora: Encounter with Salman Rushdie.* Penguin Books, 2009.

Joshi, Chandra B. *V.S. Naipaul: The Voices of Exiles.* Sterling Publishers, 1994.

Kaufman, Michael. "Author from Three Countries". *New York Times Book Review*, Nov. 13, 1983. pp. 20-24.

Mukherjee, Bharati. *Darkness.* Penguin, 1985.

Naipaul, V.S. *An Area of Darkness*. Picador, 2002.

Naipaul, V.S. *Finding the Centre*, Andrea Deutsch, 1994.

Naipaul, V.S. *India: A Million Mutinies Now*. Vintage, 1991.

Naipaul, V.S. *Reading and Writing: A Personal Account*. New York Review of Books, 2000.

Parameswaran Uma. *The Door I Shut Behind Me: Selected Fiction, Poetry and Drama,* Affiliated East-West Press, 1990.

Parameswaran Uma. *Trishanku*. Toronto South Asian Review (TSAR), 1988.

Rama, Rau Santha. *East of Home*. Harper and Brother, 1950.

Rama, Rau Santha. *Gifts of Passage*. Harper and Brother, 1961.

Rama, Rau Santha. *Home to India*. Harper and Brother, 1945.

Rathore Mahanta, Namrata. *V.S. Naipaul: The Indian Trilogy*. Atlantic Publishers & Distributors, 2004.

Ray, Mohit K. (ed.). *V.S. Naipaul: Critical Essay*, Vol. I. Atlantic Publishers & Distributors, 2002.

Ray, Mohit K. (ed.). *V.S. Naipaul: Critical Essay*, Vol. II. Atlantic Publishers & Distributors, 2002.

Rushdie, Salman. *Imaginary Homelands: Essays and Criticism*. Granta Books, 1991.

Rushdie, Salman. *Shame*. Vintage Books, 2001.

Shahid, Ali Agha. *Bone-Sculpture*. Writers Workshop, 1972.

Shahid, Ali Agha. *In Memory of Begum Akhtar.* Writers Workshop, 1979.

Shahid, Ali Agha. *The Half-Inch Himalayas*. Wesleyan University Press, 1987.

Shahid, Ali Agha. *The Nostalgist's Map of America*. W.W. Norton, 1991.

Singh, Manjit Inder. *V.S. Naipaul: Writers of the Indian Diaspora*, second edition. Rawat Publications, 2001.

Tharoor, Shashi. *The Five Dollar Smile: Fourteen Early Stories and a Farce in Two Acts*. Viking Press, 1990.

Varghese, C.P. *Nirad C. Chaudhari*. Humanities Press, 1973.

Vassanji, M.G. *No New Land*. McClelland and Stewart, 1991.

Vassanji, M.G. *The Gunny Sack*. Heinemann International, 1989.

Vassanji, M.G. *Uhuru Street*. McClelland and Stewart, 1992.

2

The Homeland Nostalgia

Nobody would argue that V.S. Naipaul is not a diasporic writer. His grandparents were a part of huge dispersal of Indians to provide indentured labor for the British Empire after the abolition of slavery. And he himself was in self-imposed exile from Trinidad, his birthplace, living in England but claiming never to feel at home anywhere. His consciousness of homelessness is at the root of his whole oeuvre, and he is always one of the first writers mentioned in any general discussion of the Indian Diaspora. One can evoke Leon Gottfried's words which capture the essence of diaspora, in trying to understand V.S. Naipaul better:

> In a century marked by political upheaval, mass migration (forced and otherwise), Colonization, revolution...it is inevitable that much modern literature should be a literature of exile. Most poignant with this category is the literature of exile *pur sang*, of the displaced or dispossessed who do not have, never have had, and, by the nature of things, never could have a home against which their condition of exile can be assessed.... [T]he writings of V.S. Naipaul draw upon an experience so totally based on layered levels of alienation and exile that his work becomes paradigmatic of the whole genre, and hence of a major current in twentieth century life, thought, and art. (Gottfried 442-43)

Naipaul's writings dealt with the cultural confusion and the problems of an outsider as an Indian in the West Indies and a West Indian in England. Though he was of a descent from laborers who came to the Caribbean from Eastern Uttar Pradesh, he thought himself to be a man without a country. Even at his young age, he was caught between his Indianness and his desire to get away from it. Suffering from his rootlessness, he looked with penetrating insight at a number of countries and this insight has hurt many countries, especially the Third World countries. In an interview published in *The Times of India*, he comments: "When people are wicked, you tell them they are wicked. If people are cruel you tell them they are cruel. If they are not aspiring and lazy, you have to tell that they have to do that—that's part of it, part of writing" (Qtd. Ray 86).

Naipaul's two books on India, *An Area of Darkness* and *India: A Wounded Civilization* reveal his hostility for the immensity and disorder of the country, crippling grasp of traditions, noticeable religiosity and the corruption of the rulers. All this provoked him to denounce India as an area of darkness. *An Area of Darkness* is Naipaul's profound reckoning with his ancestral homeland and an extraordinarily perceptive chronicle of his first encounter of his first phase of his imagination and his coming to terms with his diasporic status. He comments: "India had in a special way been the background of my childhood from which my grandfather came, a country never physically described and therefore never real, a country out in the void beyond the dot of Trinidad; and from it our journey had been final" (*AAD* 21).

For Naipaul, India has been a special country, from where his grandfather and others had come to Trinidad as indentured laborers. There were so many other people who had come along with Naipaul's paternal grandparents. Two of them were Gold Teeth Nanee and her grave husband. Their fierce loyalty to their language and the Indian way of life made them look like foreigners in Trinidad. They brought their India within them. Naipaul writes: "Half of us (Indians) on this land of the Cagunes (in Trinidad) were pretending perhaps only feeling, never formulating it as an idea that we brought a kind of India with us, which we could, as it were, unroll like a carpet on the flat land" (Qtd. Ray iv).

Naipaul's precise intention was to discover his roots and identity from which he had been alienated culturally, emotionally and by birth. His acquaintance with India was only through what he had got to know from his ancestors. From his childhood, he romanticized India and on his first visit he tried to realize the romanticized image of the land of his ancestors. Naipaul's idea of India found its way through his birth into a Hindu joint family in Trinidad. India was around him in shape of people and things since he gained consciousness. The few articles his ancestors carried from India like brass vessels, images, a ruined harmonium, a string bed, etc. were some of them. These things constituted an image of the country of his forefathers and made India for him. He writes about them with a touch of feeling: "More than in people, India lay about us in things: in a string bed or two...in innumerable brass vessels: in wooden printing blocks...in drums and one ruined harmonium in brightly colored pictures of deities on pink lotus or radiant against Himalaya snow; and all in paraphernalia of the prayer room...the images, the smooth pebbles the stick of sandalwood" (*AAD* 23).

Naipaul, thus, grew up in an extended Hindu family bound by customs and traditions, rites and rituals and always trying to protect the Indianness against the possible harmful contamination of an alien culture. The life was full of conventions. But with every generation, India became an increasingly distant object until Naipaul's India became more a legendary than a real one.

Naipaul frequently tried to impose his romanticized image of India on the reality but when the reality had gone against his pre-conceived notions, his narrative skills slipped into an unwarranted, moralizing and misplaced criticism. Naipaul comments about this symptom: "The India then which was the background of my childhood was an area of imagination. It was not the real country, and I presently began to read about and whose map I committed to memory" (*AAD* 37).

Naipaul's *A House of Mr Biswas* was an imaginative account of the Indian experience in Trinidad, especially dealing with his father's life and his own youth. A few years after its publication, he visited India for the first time and wrote his first full-fledged book on Indian—*An Area of Darkness*. He said that India had been an ancestral fascination for him and he could not get away from it.

All three books of Naipaul written in the Indian background were published at a time when Indian novels were an oddity, mainly Indian novels from West Indies. Thus, Naipaul's book suffered critical and commercial neglect. Disappointments filled Naipaul's life to a great extent. His life in London left no meaning for him. It turned to be sterile and mean. His visit to Trinidad was only to justify his early childhood days. Finally, there remained only India, the destination of his journey and the land of his forefathers. In *Reading and Writing*, Naipaul recalls this realization:

> One day deep in my almost fixed depression I began to see what my material might be: the city street from whose mixed life we had held aloof, and the country life before that, with the ways and manners of a remembered India. It seemed easy and obvious when it had been found; but it had taken me four years to see it. Almost at the same time came the language, the tone, the voice for that material. It was as if voice and matter form were part of one another. (*RW* 15)

Naipaul undertook his first visit to India with the conventional ideas of it as the land of Gandhi and Nehru, the land of glorious past (great histories and leaders), the place of honesty and dedication, truthfulness and non-violence, Vedic culture and harmony, the Brahmanic world of rites and rituals and the myths he was told in his childhood days by his forefathers. His heart filled with joy when he decided to visit the country of his dreams. He expressed his feelings for India in such a way: "As India had drawn near…some little feeling for India as the mythical land of my childhood was awakened" (*AAD* 38).

However, the fact remains that Naipaul observes a huge difference between the imagination and the reality which he was confronted with is just the opposite of the India of his imagination. He is shocked when he witnesses dirt, filth, pollution, poverty, rural society and corruption prevalent everywhere in the country. Being a Brahmin he pays much attention to the cleanliness—physical, mental and spiritual. The description of four men washing down the steps of a Bombay seedy hotel reveals Naipaul's concern towards growing caste system in the country and passes a moral comment on it. He observes:

> After they have passed, the steps are dirty as before.... You cannot complain the hotel is dirty. No Indian will agree with you. Four sweepers are in daily attendance and it is enough in India that the sweepers attend. They are not required to *clean*. This is subsidiary part of their function which is to *be* sweepers, degraded beings, to go through the motions of degradation. (*AAD* 76)

In spite of being a Brahmin, he does not favor caste-system but opposes it. He holds the view that the caste system is a curse to the humanity and proves to be a stigma on the face of the country and hence, the existing social structure needs to be changed to get a better future. On this view of Naipaul, Landeg White observes:

> His visit to the village of his grandfather, though briefly enchanting, arouses problems over language, fears about the food and water, demands for money, and concludes with Naipaul's angry refusal to give a relative a life into town. There is no home for him in India; his assumptions are too much of the west, yet just as it was in London that he wrote the Trinidad novels, viewing his background from the security of escape, so it is in Kashmir that he writes *Mr Stone and the Knights Companion*, projecting on to his English hero a strong Hindu sense of the world as illusion. Returning to Europe, he is no longer able to believe in the places in which he has lived and worked a Brahmin-cum-Englishmen in Trinidad, a European in India, an Indian in London. (White 7)

Naipaul has portrayed the picture of India through his characters, an India with a human associations rather than a castiest obligation, an India which will utilize the bravery, honesty, and skills to build a better nation beyond of all social and national prejudices. According to him, the common efforts of the majority of India will pave country's way towards progress and will help to build nation's future in a healthy way.

Naipaul's *India: A Million Mutinies Now* is an account of the experience of the people of its own country. It holds the response of Indian people to its own history, culture and civilization. Sometimes people meet unexpected sense of guilt and repent. Sometimes they make an attempt to amend and rectify to get things well and another time they are filled with a sense of fulfillment and satisfaction. On the whole, the characters described in *India: A Million Mutinies Now* set in Indian background, display a development and a stream of consciousness of their history, a desire to adapt and change, and an ability to analyze their own history rationally. Naipaul completely accedes to the situation described in the book. Dilip Padgaonkar reports on Naipaul's view: "There is a big historical development going on in India, wise men should understand it and ensure that it does not remain in the hands of fantasies. Rather they should use it for the intellectual transformation of India" (Padgaonkar 10).

Naipaul's inability to be associated with any of the living society makes his identity as a displaced person. It makes him to think of homelessness as a universal feature. Though he is connected with three different societies by birth and education, he fails to establish any living contact with any of them. He describes his detachment with England and considers India as his true home. His feeling is similar to that of R. Parthasarathy who remarks: "A part of me finally died in England. Should I have the journey at all? It had broken my life into two" (Parthasarathy 66).

Naipaul admits that his return to India after twenty-seven years has been different from his visit in 1962. He thinks that his Indian nerve has helped him abolishing the darkness that separated him from his ancestral past. He writes: "I had carried in my bones that idea of abjectness and defeat and shame [his ancestors had left as indentured servants for the sugar estates of Guyana and Trinidad]. It was the idea I had taken to India on that slow journey by train and ship in 1962: it was the source of my nerves" (*MMN* 602).

Naipaul's emotional attachment with India shows the deep agony of his heart which he comes across time to time through his writings, written in the background of India. Finally, he finds his roots in the same country for which he was wandering all over the world. He takes pride in coming originally from the family which had its roots in India. Whatever he was told about India, was enough to arouse in him a sense of emotional involvement. His visit to India was the result of his feelings for it. Naipaul's early attitude and later transformation become more understandable when we examine the circumstances of his life, which made him an outsider wherever he went. In an interview with Dilip Padgaonkar for the *Times of India*, he says: "I do not have the tenderness more secure people can have towards bush people…I feel threatened by them. My attitude and the attitude of the people like me is quite different from the people who live outside the bush or who just go camping in the bush on weekends" (Padgaonkar 10).

Naipaul's return to India time and again and his minute and detailed study of the Indian heritage, cultural variety, its landscape and its people show that he is optimistic about the future of India. He truly appreciates the courage of people and admits the necessity of freedom movement, when the country was suffering from the dark ages of invasions and wars. Such movements, he maintains, helped people of India to awaken and let them think of their duties to perform and this spirit of liberation took its shape in the form of rage, protest and revolt. In this way, India has turned into a land of million mutinies now, which marked the beginning of self-, the beginning of intellectual life—a life which finds its focus in the idea of a strong nation. These mutinies can be regarded as the liberating forces which become necessary towards India's growth and its restoration. If the people holding prominent places in the country encourage the lower level people to protest and discourage the evils existing in the social and political system of the country, the winds of change blow and the change takes the shape of disturbance, nevertheless, it is a precursor of real growth.

Shanti Shivaraman aptly observes in this connection: "After the dark ages of invasion, vandalism and wars, the freedom movement which led to the independence of India symbolizes to Naipaul "the truest kind of liberation". It has awakened people to knowledge of who they are and what they owe themselves" (Shivaraman 38).

Naipaul's *India: A Million Mutinies Now* is also a record of Naipaul's visit to different places of India and it starts with his journey to Delhi and Amritsar. He begins his journey with a description of Bombay. His journey across Bombay brings him in contact with different classes and sections of the society. He witnesses the celebration of Ambedkar's birthday by a huge crowd of Dalits. To him, it is a sign of awakening and . These people are full of confidence and are ready to initiate change. Shanti Shivaraman states: "This homage paid to a great man becomes a moment of triumph and honor to the men and women who had joined the celebration—an awakening of intelligence, knowledge and honour. Theof their particularity and the courage to assert themselves are signs of confidence and change" (Shivaraman 138).

The alienated sections of the society form their groups and each group derives its strength from different sources, like the harijans (depressed class of the society) derive their inspiration from Dr. B.R. Ambedakar and the middle-class Hindus derive their strength from the worship of the God Ganesh. Thus, Naipaul finds different people representing the different sections and sub-sections of society. Namrata Rathore Mahanta remarks how the writer records his transformation: "With *India: A Million Mutinies Now*, Naipaul overcomes his obsession with his response to India and looks at the country through the eyes of its people. Thus, the Naipaulian shift from the self to the country across twenty-seven years finds its narrative equivalent in his book on India (Rathore Mahanta 116).

It is very clear that Naipaul has mixed feelings about India. On one hand, India is the land, spiritually and physically, of his ancestors. On the other hand, it is a reminder of the poverty and desolation that his ancestors 'escaped' from to make a new life in Trinidad. It is, as with many people of Indian ancestry who are brought up abroad, Naipaul grew up with the idea of a united India, a land of one people and one culture, but on his first visit to India this idea was shattered. As he explores the land of his forefathers, he discovers that in India, being 'Indian' is not enough. State language, religion, caste, sub-caste, family, village, etc. are all important in terms of how a person fits in with the world. Thus, despite the fact that he was brought up with some exposure to at least some aspects of the food, language (some of the women in his family at least probably spoke a little Hindi), culture and religion (Hinduism) of India, Naipaul has a good enough distance to be able to make insightful observations about India but a difficult thing is that occasionally a glimpse of his resentment and complicated feelings about India do come in and perhaps affect his judgment. Naipaul states: "In 27 years I had succeeded in making a kind of return, shedding my Indian nerves. Abolishing the darkness that separated me from my ancestral past" (*MMN* 602).

India: A Million Mutinies Now was written after Naipaul had made a few trips to India, and it is clear that he has come to terms with same kinds of the alienation that assailed him on his first visit. He seems mostly at ease moving around between different states and cities and also has many contacts whom he calls upon from time to time. He occasionally recalls his previous experiences though. On the other hand, although he may be more used to India, he is not really reconciled to certain aspects of India and her people. It is evident that he retains quite a bit frustration for the way that Indian people think and act. However, it must be pointed that his frustration and desire for India and its people is clearly an indication of his deep-seated affection for the country. Here in this context it is appropriate to say that Naipaul expresses his annoyance at various weaknesses in India because he seems to be worried for her well-being. Namrata Rathore Mahanta comments: "Naipaul's third book on India, *India: A Million Mutinies Now* marks the third stage in Naipaul's engagement with India. In this book Naipaul has analyzed and explained the construction of his own first response to India. The book is a picture gallery of India" (Rathore Mahanta 120).

Naipaul's third book on India changed his vision completely and he tried to be insightful. This book is a collection of interviews and interactions with various people from different areas of India, as Naipaul travels around, sometimes going back to places he has been and people he has met on previous trips. He has a knack for interviewing some very interesting people and he lets them tell their stories as they see them. Also, he does provide his own analysis, which he uses to back up with his own theories. Thus, the overall theme of the book is about the changes that India has gone through and continues to go through. It is evident in this work that Naipaul is unhappy with many of the changes. Another theme is the way the mini revolutions or 'mutinies' of different communities in India which are going on. For instance are the Pro-Dravidian movement in the south and the various communist movements in the North East. The picture the book paints is of a country with many different groups of people who do not always find it easy to get along and often feel that they must try and make the country and define their place in it. Naipaul has been extremely successful in interpreting those changing times in Indian history. He has given a thoughtful introduction to what India means to its population of Jains, Hindus, Muslims, Sikhs and others. He has insightfully deciphered the role of class, caste, religion, and region in the making of a new and stronger India contrary to the belief. He establishes the argument that diversity is the new India's biggest strength and perhaps a major cause of democratic success. His journey ends with the realization that many small and large mutinies among the various castes, religion and areas of India are helpful to regain its important position among other countries: Naipaul writes:

> In the 130 years or so since the mutiny—the last 90 years of the British Raj and the first 40 years of independence begin increasingly to appear as part of the same historical period—the idea of freedom has gone everywhere in India.... The liberation of spirit that has come to India could not come as release alone. In India, with its layer below layer

> of distress and cruelty, it had to come as rage and revolt. India was now a country of million mutinies. (*MMN* 605)

Naipaul sees possibilities for regeneration in the nascent freedom. His 'Trilogy' presents a collection of people from different parts of India, different classes, caste and religion. He attempts to find out what drives them within the wider social context and how they see themselves, their values and their expectations and how they are standing up to the changing time. His portraits are clear, from a former Naxalite leader from south, to a former Nawab of Lucknow, gangster from Bombay, a disillusioned Sikh, and a Bengali Boxwallah. An access into the minds of such a wide range of people is definitely the best thing portrayed by Naipaul. Thus, the mutinies become a means of restoration and Naipaul points out:

> Excess was now felt to be excess India. What the mutinies were also helping to define was the strength of the general intellectual life, and the wholeness and humanism of the values to which all Indians now felt they could appeal. And—strange irony—the mutinies were not to be wished away. They were part of the beginning of a new way for many millions. Part of India's growth part of its restoration. (*MMN* 604).

Naipaul hopes that million mutinies, supported by twenty kinds of "group excess, sectarian excess, religious, excess, regional excess" (*MMN* 603), would seem as the beginning of general growth in the intellectual life of Indian citizens. His discussions with various people, their opinions though confused are connected with the country. Naipaul's own understanding as a displaced person makes it possible to have a border perspective about the several views concerning the country and says that as he moves from satire and contempt towards sympathy, love, affection and understanding of India, Indian people with its sections, class, divisions and categories moves in the direction of possibilities, growth and, then development. Landeg White opines: "Identity is at odds with their society, who understands homelessness and the threat of disorder, who feel condemned permanently to provincialism, who are ready to sympathize with struggle and failure and triumph" (White 126).

Naipaul talks to various people across country, understanding the views and opinions of the country's people. He meets people who are optimistic, who lead a fearful life and for whom Dr. Babasaheb Ambedkar the man, who freed them from the captivity of untouchability, is a deity. As he continues his journey to the other parts of the country, he meets Rajan, a displaced Brahmin in Calcutta; Kala, a Tamil woman who has thrown off the traditions; Dipanjan, a science professor in West Bengal; Rashid, a Shia Muslim in Lucknow and Gurtej, a Sikh in Chandigarh and many more. But at the end of the book *India: A Million Mutinies Now*, the author's following line summarizes his experience during his visit to India: "Change is present everywhere" (*MMN* 603).

Naipaul broadly writes about many reforms running through the country in agriculture, industry and living standards. He describes the electrification in villages, irrigation system in agriculture and sanitary improvements in slums. The Indian scientific growth and development is also no less important. India is slowly recovering from its failures. The intellectual capacity of the country is increasing and the new technological centers are established like space research and the aircraft industry in Bangalore.

Naipaul is deeply concerned with the changes in social structure. Indians, like people in other countries strive, hard to improve their standards of living. Education is very important for them and many young people go to finish their studies at the universities abroad.

Thus, the book presents how people continue to be victorious in spite of the chaos, untidiness and poverty. It is a travelogue with an analogy between the emancipation of millions and the mutiny of 1857. The book is somewhat optimistic about the country and its people.

What makes Naipaul's Indian trilogy interesting is the uniqueness of Naipaul's position itself. He was born and grew up in Trinidad, where his grandfather came as an indentured servant from India. Young Naipaul left Trinidad to finish his studies at Oxford and he permanently settled in England. His Indian origins, Trinidadian birth and British citizenship allow him to see Indian people from a considerably different perspective. He is an 'insider' as well as 'outsider' to India. Through his Indian ancestry he can see the country from a very intimate point of view, whereas his foreignness helps him keep more detached position for his observation. However, this kind of double perspective makes it more difficult for Naipaul to understand his own feeling and reactions in some of the situations that he has to face in India, especially when he realizes his own strangeness. Sometimes he seems surprised by the revelation of his demerits that he was not aware of. For Naipaul, the cognition of India is simultaneously the discovery of himself.

In the whole trilogy, the reader may notice V.S. Naipaul's experiments with his narrative techniques as well as his changing attitude towards India. It must be taken into consideration that the books were written over a long period of time, specifically within almost thirty years, so that India itself did not remain unchanged. Most of the twists of Naipaul's attitude to the country arise from the changes of India and its people. His Trinidadian childhood, Indian origin and the residency in London make his position in the world highly undetermined. He cannot fully identify with any of these countries. He rather sees himself as a blend of the three cultures. He feels absolutely alienated and unable to identify with any of these societies.

WORKS CITED

Gottfried, Leon. "Preface: The Face of V.S. Naipaul". *Modern Fiction Studies*. Autumn, 1984.

Naipaul, V.S. *An Area of Darkness*. Picador, 2002.

Naipaul, V.S. *India: A Million Mutinies Now*. Vintage, 1991.

Naipaul, V.S. *Reading and Writing: A Personal Account*, New York Review of Books, 2000.

Padgaonkar, Dilip. "An Area of Awakening", *The Times of India*, July 19, 1993. pp. 8-12.

Parthasarathy, R. "Whoring after English Gods." Guy Amirthanayagam (ed.), *Writers in East-West Encounter*, Palgrave Macmillan, 1982. pp. 65-68.

Rathore Mahanta, Namrata. *V.S. Naipaul: The Indian Trilogy.* Atlantic Publishers and Distributors, 2004.

Ray, Mohit K. (ed). *V.S. Naipaul: Critical Essays,* Vol. I. Atlantic Publishers and Distributors, 2002.

Singh, Rahul. *Times News Network*. *Times of India*, Oct. 13, 2001, p. 21.

Sivaraman, Shanti. "V.S. Naipaul's *India: A Million Mutinies Now*—A Celebration." Mohit K. Ray (ed.), *V.S. Naipaul: Critical Essays*, Vol. II, Atlantic Publishers and Distributors, 2002. pp. 135-42.

White, Landeg. *V.S. Naipaul.* Macmillan Press Ltd., 1975.

3
Social Ethos

Naipaul is a West Indian novelist but with an Indian background which becomes a part of a mixed culture. The West Indian culture is the product of his cultural displacement. Thus, he tries to escape from his dependence and moves from the extreme stage of nostalgia to the extreme stage of imagination. Naipaul comments in this connection, "Living in a borrowed culture, the West Indian, more than most, needs writers to tell him, who he is and where he stands" (*MP* 73).

Naipaul maintains that his attitude to Hinduism is ambivalent. Being an Indian Brahmin uprooted from the lands of his forefathers, he judges the worth of Indian life and culture with the Hindu standard of *karma*, *dharma* and *moksha*. However, he claims that his approach is of a non-believer Hindu, who is completely unaware of the tenets of Hinduism, though he has to witness many rituals. Evidence of his deep-rooted Brahmin upbringing and his resilient agnosticism can be understood from the following lines in which he says:

> I come of a family that abounded with pundits. But I had born an unbeliever. I took no pleasure in religious ceremonies. They were too long and food only came at the end. I didn't understand the language—it was as if our elders expected our understanding would be instinctive and no one explained the prayers or the ritual.... My uncle often put it to me that my denial was an admissible type of Hinduism. Examining myself I found only that sense of the difference of people, which I have tried to explain,

> a vague sense of caste, and a horror of the unclean. (*MP* 88-89)

Naipaul believes that his Hindu upbringing has left in him an indistinct sense of caste and hatred of unclean.

Thus, it is noteworthy that Naipaul himself was surprised at his Hindu-based childhood and his youth in the diversified culture of Trinidad. He himself amazes at the deep-rooted Hinduism in him and expresses:

> That this world should have existed at all, even in the unconsciousness of a child, it is to me a marvel, as it is a marvel that we sound have accepted the separateness of our juxtaposition. In one world we existed as if in blinkers, as if seeing no more than my grandfather's village; outside we were totally self-aware. And in India, I want to see that not many of the things which the newer and how perhaps truer side of my nature kicked against—the smugness, as it seemed to me the double-talk and double-think had an answer in that side of a myself I had thought buried and which Indian received as a faint memory I understood than I admitted. (*AAD* 30)

Naipaul gives the background of his Hindu childhood and its proof is the reference to 'Katha,' the Indian cultural form arranged in Trinidad at the passionate wish of his grandmother. He narrates:

> My grandmother wished to have a 'Katha' said, and she wished to have it said under a Pipal tree. There was only one Pipal tree in the Island, it was in the Botanical gardens. Permission was applied for. To my amazement it was given; and on one Sunday morning, we all sat under a Pipal tree, botanically labelled and the pundit read. The crackling sacrificial fire was scented with pitch-pine, brown sugar and ghee; bells were rung, gongs struck, conch shells blown. We attracted the salient interest of a small mixed crowd of morning strollers and proselytizing attentions of a Seventh Day Adventist. It was a scene of a pure pastoral: Aryan ritual, of another continent and age, a few hundred yards from the governor's house. (*AAD* 26-27)

Born in a traditional Brahmin family Naipaul knew the relevance of sacrifice. He discloses the continuing impact of sacrifice on Hindu self. Naipaul writes the importance of sacrifices in the life he perceives:

> I know, for instance, the beauty of sacrifice so important to the Aryans. Sacrifice turned the cooking of food into a ritual: first cooked thing usually a small round of unleavened bread, a miniature, especially, especially made—was always for the fire, the god. This was possible only with an open fireplace; to have to give up the customs, if I attempt now to expand on what to a child was only a passing sense of wrongness was to abjure a link with the earth and the antiquity of the earth, the beginning of things. (*IWC* 11)

Naipaul has always been conscious of the rituals performed one after another in the family. He was totally aware of the customs that his family used to perform. Sometimes the customs of his childhood were mysterious. For example, the cutting of a pumpkin with a male hand seemed to him at one point to have some sexual connotation in the rite. But the truth was somewhat a revelation for him as he had it at the end of in *India: A Wounded Civilization* when Naipaul came to know that:

> The pumpkin in Bengal and in adjoining areas is a vegetable substitute for a living sacrifice; the male hand was therefore necessary. In India, I know, I am stranger, but increasingly I understand that my Indian memories, the memories of that Indian which lived into my childhood in Trinidad are 'like trapdoors into a bottomless past'. (*IWC* 12)

Naipaul's Hindu upbringing has left such a deep impression on him that he bursts into anger when he comes to know that in Bombay people used candles and electric bulbs for the Diwali festival and not the rustic clay lamps, which his family still used in Trinidad.

Naipaul presents an experience, which he encounters in the course of bus ride from Awantipur to Srinagar. When the bus, hired by a large tourist family, halts to have a break from sight-seeing to eat, Naipaul is also offered food and he minutely watches the ritualistic way in which the food is being served. He experiences a sense of incredible closeness and understanding with the group. Though the food is served with dirty hands, Naipaul doesn't feel it is unclean despite him being acutely aware how some people can be unclean. All such habits (being too conscious and insistent on cleanliness) are ingrained in him because of his Brahmin upbringing. Naipaul unpacks a detailed observation of the event:

> They were a Brahmin family and their vegetarian food was served according to established form. No one was allowed to touch it except the dirty old servant who, at the mention of food, had been kindled into such important activity. With the very fingers that a moment before had been rolling a crinkled cigarette and had then seized the dusty Dalda tins from off the dusty bus floor, he now—using only the right hand, of course—distributed puris from one tin, scooped out curried potatoes from another, and from a third secured dripping fingerfuls of chutney. (*AAD* 147-48)

On meeting this family, Naipaul feels that he is at home in India. But when he meets another family he tells: "The people I had met in Delhi clubs and Bombay flats the villagers and officials in country distract were strangers whose background I could not read" (*AAD* 149).

Naipaul's visits to India confirm that the land of his childhood remains an area of darkness for him. His journey through the land of his forefathers only confirms his separateness from India. However, Naipaul's visit to the village of Dubes to meet the members of his grandfather's family marks a sense of joy, when he describes the village:

> It was set for back from the embankment. It exceeded anything I had expected. A large mango groove gave it a pastoral aspects, and two spires showed white and clean against the dark green foliage. I knew about those spires and was glad to see them. My grandfather had sought to re-establish the family he had left behind in India. He had recovered their land; he had given money for the building of a temple. No temple had been built, only three shrines.

> Poverty, fecklessness, we had thought in Trinidad. But now, from the road how reassuring those spires were. (*AAD* 275)

But when Naipaul meets Ram Chandra Dube, he is disappointed seeing the poverty in latter's life. His early happiness turns into a sense of loss and feels eager to leave when Ram Chandra asks for financial help telling that his grandfather's land is now reduced to only nine acre. Naipaul wants to go back and cannot deal successfully with the guilt of being responsible for Ram Chandra's fate. Thus, his visit to his ancestral village and meeting Dube is altogether a disappointing experience and fails to give him any fruitful connection between his Brahmin-self in India.

D.J. Enright observes that Naipaul has the sensibility of a Brahmin but not the supporting belief and his writings on India show that the Brahmin sensibility has been overlaid with a Western vision and as a result of which there is a no home for him in India. When his Brahmin sensibility relates his experience in India to what he had experienced as a boy when he was in Trinidad, Naipaul finds security and happiness belonging to the country and having a home. But whenever he fails to relate to the reality, Naipaul tends to attack India with a Western mindset, with a Western point of view. He comments with a feeling of despair: "It is fundamental to the understanding of India's intellectual second-ratedness which is generally taken for granted but may be the most startling and depressing fact about the world's second most populous country, which now has little to offer the world except its Gandhian concept of holy poverty and the recurring crooked comedy of its holy men" (*IWC* 92).

Naipaul's dual personality, as an Indian and westerner at once in India, has generated all the problems. He has a Western outlook towards Indians and seems to speak on behalf of England at times. His happiness, exhilaration, exaltation and amusements derive simultaneously from his Brahmin-self and his inherent Western outlook. At the end of *An Area of Darkness*, Naipaul confesses that his duality thwarts his attempt to capture the essence of India.

Naipaul's comments on Hindus disclose that inner Hindu world emphasizes caste rules. Caste and classes are the important factors dominating social customs in India. Hindus have to abide by the rules laid down by the casteist societies. The stiff caste groupings and the concept of "*karma*" cause in Indian society a distressing acceptance of social injustice. Sharada Iyer writes in this connection:

> Caste was a medieval tyranny, using religious sanctions and psychologically imprinting to preserve the fundamental Status Quo and for the lowest of castes abolishing the essential sense of individual esteem and personal dignity. It is this aspect of the caste which is exposed in V.S. Naipaul's mordant irritable but accurately observant study of his travels in India, *An Area of Darkness*. Naipaul in spite of his Brahminical background couldn't understand nor accept the religious consciousness or religious view of life, surely the consequences of his markedly western background. (Qtd. Ray 89)

Naipaul presents a penetrating analysis of Manohar Malgonkar's *The Princes* to illustrate Indian caste system. *The Princes*, the narrative of Indian petty prince losing power with independence and feeling the humiliations of his fall very deeply and going out unarmed after a wounded tiger and died, is really a tragedy. But here Naipaul's chief focus is not the prince, however the prince too, hails from casteless Deccani bandits, who surrendered a lakh of rupees to the pundits in exchange for caste privileges when they obtained political power. The prince is against encouragement of the lower classes represented by the untouchable Kanakchand. To Naipaul, it is natural in a person of the historical role and power.

Abhayaraj, the prince's son and his half-brother Charudatt are the students in a local primary school and are kept away from the untouchables in the school. Untouchables sit on the floor at the back and watch the day-to-day school activities from a distance. Abhayaraj makes Kanakchand a friend in school and writes an essay as a competition entry for him. Kanakchand is awarded the first prize but when the truth of his Dalit identity is disclosed and the prize is snatched away from him. Kanakchand gets a beating with a stick for lying and cheating but Abhayaraj supports Kanakchand in his studies by helping him to get a scholarship. Naipaul says that Kanakchand was his "first direct contact with the quivering poverty of India" (*AAD* 64). Kanakchand's poverty really disheartens Naipaul as he describes his lunch is "one black roti, chillies and an onion" (*AAD* 66). Naipaul finds poverty nowhere described in its reality by Malgonkar in *The Princes*.

Naipaul finds most Hindus as people with similar insensitivity and callousness borne of a caste perspective and rigid caste code as in Abhayaraj. Naipaul also discovers the case of Ramnath—the steno in a government department and Hiralal the typist to reveal the caste system of India. The designated steno Ramnath denies to type in short hand in spite of his university-educated boss Malhotra's threats to dismiss him; he does not agree to take dictation or type as it is not his but Hiralal's job. Naipaul observes:

> ...the man who makes a dingy bed in the hotel room will be affronted if he is asked to sweep the gritty floor. The clerk will not bring you a glass of water even if you faint. The architecture student will consider it a degradation to make drawings, to be a mere draughtsman. And Ramnath the stenographer, so designated on a triangular block of wood that stands on his desk, will refuse to type out what he has taken down in shorthand. (*AAD* 45)

For Naipaul: "...a knowledge of degree is in the bones and no Indian is far from his origins. It is like physical a yearning" (*AAD* 54).

Naipaul admits that he has grown to see caste as only a limited part of his personal life. Citing an example from his Trinidad days, he recollects a marriage, where it was rumored that the husband was of a 'leather-work caste'. The man held an eminent position of some responsibility. He was wealthy enough and had travelled far and wide but he was from a lower caste. However, Naipaul says it was a rumor.

He comes to know really about caste whenever he meets up people in India. Naipaul thinks about Indian people that they are contaminated by their caste especially when it is known publicly in advance whether approvingly or disapprovingly. Naipaul remarks:

> But caste in Indian was not what it had been to me in Trinidad. In Trinidad caste had no meaning in our day-to-day life; the caste we occasionally played at was no more than an acknowledgement of latent qualities; the assurance it offered was such as might have been offered by a palmist or a reader of handwriting. In India it implied a brutal division of labor; at its center, as I had never realized, lay the degradation of the latrine-cleaner. In India caste was unpleasant; I never wished to know what a man's caste was. (*AAD* 28-29)

Naipaul has unmitigated disregard for the upper class uneducated Hindu families, who are very fond of foreign articles. The example of such type is Mrs. Mahindra, the wife of Delhi contractor. Naipaul gets a rented room in Mrs. Mahindra's house, where he finds everything imported except for the brass-dish warmer. However, Naipaul credits her kindness in welcoming him.

Naipaul further considers it as a pitiable condition of the scheduled caste people when they are looked down upon by the upper class people. Though the scheduled caste citizens enjoy special privilege on account of reservation, their position is far from being comfortable. They are not accepted by the mainstream society. He observes that untouchability has not been uprooted completely from the minds of the upper class people.

Naipaul quests for an identity. This quest is made difficult because of contempt and critique for India which in turn is a result of his British citizenship. Despite being a Hindu Brahmin, he is not at all interested in rites and rituals and he tries to find his imagined India. Rather unfortunately, with the mixture of British citizenship, he does not find comfort in distress and remains homeless without any identity. Naipaul writes about his problems with mindless rituals: "I had no belief; I disliked religious rituals; and I had a sense of ridiculous. I refused to go through the *Janaywa*, or thread ceremony of the newborn, with some of my cousins. The ceremony ends with the initiate, his head shaved.... So I refused; though now this ancient drama, absurdly surviving in a Trinidad yard, seems to me touching and attractive" (*AAD* 29).

Presenting his views at the symposium on the East Indians in the Caribbean at the university of West Indies in June 1975, on the topic—The Question of the identity of the East Indian in the Caribbean, Naipaul has said that there was an ignorance of the Indian community not only from without, but also from within in West Indies. Naipaul said that Indians had to think about the culture from which they had come and hence that was why the subject of identity became more difficult. The large Indian community came to the Caribbean were from the peasantry who were unable to be touched by the great reform movements of India in nineteenth century. Such reform movements were a response to British rule and ideas and Indian emigrants, by forgetting their rich past, were adding to their distress in the Caribbean. Naipaul states that Indians in Trinidad come from culture that had not been given to self-examination or to historical inquiry.

Naipaul was born 15 years before the independence of India and he grew up having two ideas of India—one, the India from which his forefathers had come and the second was the India of great name and great civilization and great classical legacy. Naipaul explains these two Indias in *India: A Million Mutinies Now*:

> I grew up with two ideas of India. The first idea—not one I wanted to go into too closely—was about the kind of country from which my ancestors had come.... There was a second India. It balanced the first. This second India was the India of the great civilization and the great classical past. It was the India by which, in all the difficulties of our circumstances, we felt supported. It was an aspect of our identity, the community identity we had developed,

> which, in multi-racial Trinidad had become more like a racial identity.... This was the identity I took to India on my first visit in 1962. And when I got there I found it had no meaning in India. The idea of an Indian community—in effect, a continental idea of our own Indian identity—made sense only when the community was very small, a minority, and isolated. (*MMN* 8-9)

Sometimes Naipaul praises Gandhi on the ground of sanitation and at times he finds faults with Gandhi and praises Nehru. But it was only Gandhi not Nehru who clearly saw that what was wrong with India. T.R.S. Sharma further comments in this connection, underlining Naipaul's view on Gandhi: "Sanitation was linked to caste, caste to callousness, inefficiency and hopelessly divided country, division to weakness, weakness to foreign rule. This is what Gandhi saw and no one purely of India could have seen it. It needed the straight simple vision of the West" (Sharma 25-35). Naipaul further holds a view that cleanliness or the idea of sanitation is the result of the Western vision and he narrates:

> I had seen Indian villages: the narrow, broken lanes with green slime in the gutters, the chocked back-to-back mud houses, the jumble of filth and food, animals and people, the baby in the dust, swollen bellied, black with flies, but wearing its good luck amulet. I had seen the starved child defecating at the roadside while the mangy dogs waited to eat the excrement. (*AAD* 42)

Naipaul emphasizes on the dirt and defecation as if it was a 'Eureka' to him, though it is an inherent evil in India. He is mostly preoccupied with this dirt and defecation. Once again he accuses Indians for living in squalor:

> India is the poorest country in the world. Therefore, to see its poverty is to make an observation of no value; ...You might have seen more: the smiles on faces on the begging children, their domestic groups among the pavement sleepers waking in the cool Bombay morning, father, mother and baby in a trinity of love.... You will agree; but deep down there will be annoyance; it will seem to run you then,

> too, that they are seeing only the obvious; and it will not please you to find your sensibility so accurately parodied. (*AAD* 42)

British critic William Walsh too agrees with other critics that Naipaul's return to India is as much a research into himself as into another country. He also attacks the writers and journalists who depict a distorted picture of the country that time. On one hand, he appreciates Stedman, the writer and the journalist but on the other, he criticizes the other irresponsible journalists. He condemns them strongly for their defective and manipulative reporting. In *India: A Wounded Civilization*, he says:

> Indian newspapers reflect this limited vision, this absence of inquiry, the absence of what can be called human interest. The pre-censorship liveliness of the Indian press—of what foreign observers have spoken—was confined to the editorial pages. Elsewhere there were mainly communiques, handouts, reports of speeches and functions. Indian journalists developed no reporting tradition; it often reported on India as on a foreign country. An unheadlined item from *The Statesman*, 17 September 1975:
>
> *Woman jumps to death*: A woman jumped to death after throwing her two children into a well at Chennapatna, 60 km from Bangalore recently, according to police—PTI. (*IWC* 117)

Naipaul describes his journey through India and presents his experiences in a very graphic manner. Having arrived at Bombay, he travels as far North as Kashmir, East to Calcutta and South to Madras. He meets different people and visits different places in India. He takes a pilgrimage to a holly cave in the Himalayas and stays on the Dal Lake. He describes the places, people and incidents with the novelist's perception and sense of comedy. Thus, in describing both people and places, Naipaul seems to have an insightful sight to see through them. Naipaul's characters—Kadir, Bashir, Aziz, Ali, Mohammad, Mr. Butt and Khasamah—clearly and skillfully show Naipaul's reading of Muslims and his narrations of places give complete details of Indian social, political and geographical realities. However, he is not sympathetic enough in describing India. Sometimes, he is critical and his approach is of an Englishman. Though Naipaul has a penetrating eye to look into the places and people, the image he gets and shows in his book is not the correct one according to many critics. His critical eyes are clouded with the Western spectacles. It is probably so because it is a painful experience of a homeless, rootless man without a country who is without religion, without set beliefs and values of life. Naipaul is both a non-resident Indian and a westerner though the westerner personality is pre-dominant when he presents lopsided picture of India. In his choice of the title—*An Area of Darkness*, there seems to be the influence of his English critically objective identity. In his writings on India, he whole heartedly expresses his feelings and photographically describes the experience of India. He has also revealed his expatriate sensibility in the book. Naipaul also points out the existing social evils in the society. He tells that money makes people dumb because when money speaks all else keeps quiet and he observes:

> India had changed; it was not a good and a stable country as it had once been. In the days of freedom movement, political workers, honoring Gandhi, had worn homespun as an emblem of sacrifice and service, their oneness with the poor. Now the politician's homespun stood for power. With the industrialization and economic growth people had forgotten old reverences. Men honored only money then. The great investment in development over three or four decades had led only to this, to corruption to the criminalization of polities. In seeking to rise, India had undone itself. No one is sure of anything now; all was fluid. Policeman, thief, politicians: the roles had become, interchangeable. (*MMN* 4-5)

Thus, Naipaul maintains that during recent four decades the development has been hijacked by corruption and which further has led to the criminalization of political system of the county. This present embarrassing difficult situation is not new, according to him. Its roots lay in past. In India, there have been problems: some of them are poverty, over population, superstitions, separatism and official corruption. Today the corruption has assumed the status of formality or courtesy. It seems nothing wrong in accepting bribe. It has taken a place in everyone's life and it can be found everywhere. There are other problems too such as the ruthless and authoritarian government. Naipaul observes that this situation is worse than the colonial rule. Thus, Naipaul exposes the neo-colonial tendencies in India with his outsider's objective distance from the society and systems.

WORKS CITED

Iyer, N. Sharada. "Naipaul's *India—An Area of Darkness*", Mohit K. Ray (ed.), *V.S. Naipaul Critical Essays*, Vol. II, Atlantic Publishers and Distributors, 2002. pp. 85-95.

Naipaul, V.S. *An Area of Darkness*, Picador, 2002.

Naipaul, V.S. *India: A Million Mutinies Now*, Vintage Books, 1991.

Naipaul, V.S. *India: A Wounded Civilization*, Picador, 2002.

Naipaul, V.S. *The Middle Passage*, Penguin, 1967.

Naipaul, V.S. *The Overcrowded Barracoon and other Articles*, Andre Deustch, 1972.

4
Cultural Cross-Currents

"Indian interpretations of their history are almost as painful as the history itself; and it is especially painful to see the earlier squalor being repeated today.... India, it seems will never cease, to require the arbitration of a conqueror" (*AAD* 216). Naipaul's bitter comments, like the one cited above, on the historical degeneration of India spring from his disillusionment. He feels that Indians are not scientific in writing and interpreting history and that their historical sense is largely propelled by fantasy. He finds it difficult to believe that Indians of Vedic period possessed knowledge of aircraft, telephone and atom bomb, as it is popularly claimed. He refuses to accept that they even had knowledge of surgery and every village during this period was a self-governing entity. For Naipaul such claims are not easy to accept. He reads a statement written on the notice board of a temple in Vijaynagar: "Once, after the Raja had prayed, there was 'rain of gold'; this, in India was history" (*AAD* 219). He expresses the view that such statements do not make credible history.

Naipaul comments on Indian civilization are very harsh and he does not accept the point that India ever had an aristocracy. He holds an opinion that Indians lack depth and they do not possess any original skillset to perform their work effectively. They lack creativity. They have borrowed all the disciplines and skills as they have no native tradition of critically evaluating their gains and losses. Naipaul further states about the Indian civilization that: "All the disciplines and skills that India now seeks to exercise are borrowed. Even the ideas Indians have of the achievement of their civilization are essentially the ideas given to them by European scholars in the nineteenth century" (Qtd. Ray 100).

Naipaul says that Indians consider their talent a combination of "Pre-British past" (*IWC* 112) and the "Moslem Dominance" (*IWC* 112). This clearly reveals their pride in "cultural synthesis". Indian painting was an art of princely courts (Hindu or Moslem), and was also the reflection of culture and tradition of such courts. But with the coming of the Britishers in the nineteenth century, this tradition could not survive. Painting becomes good if their patrons allow it to be. And with the arrival of the British, there were new patrons of limited interest because a new vision of looking at 'art and craft' is imposed on the Indian artists according to their new patrons. Naipaul remarks about Indian artists and the changes that they have undergone under the influence of European art:

> A new way of looking is imposed, and Indian artists become ordinary as they depict native 'types' in as European manner as their techniques allow, or when, suppressing their own idea of their function as craftsmen, their own feeling for design and organization, they struggle for what must have been for them the meaninglessness of constable-like 'views'. A vigorous art becomes imitative, second-rate, insecure (always with certain regional exceptions); it knows it cannot compete; it withers away, and is finally abolished by the camera. It is as though, in a conquered Europe, with all of European art abruptly disregarded, artists were required to paint genre pictures in, say, a Japanese manner. It can be done, but the strains will kill. (*IWC* 112-13)

What Naipaul speaks about Indian painting is also true about the Indian architecture. He finds that this tradition has also been broken. In India, modern buildings are being built year by year but the modern air conditioners have taken the place of the old ideas of ventilation. The result is disastrous. So the architects need to design the buildings suitable for the difficult climates. He regards Indian architecture as another imported skill and a part of someone else's tradition. Consequently, this art also becomes a combination of misapplied technology and misunderstood modern designs. At the same time he mentions about Indian classical dance that has regained its position, but the painting remains badly mixed in traditions and cannot achieve the same value. Consequently, Indian past can no more provide encouragement to its present, at least in painting. Naipaul once again appreciates Western artistic vision and mentions that because of its dominance and variation, Indians continue to imitate it as their skills are rooted in nothing, having given up the native traditions. He reveals India's inability to amalgamate and incorporate with other cultures and to take their artistic traditions forward, and comments:

> India, without its own living tradition, has lost the ability to incorporate and adapt; what it borrows it seeks to swallow whole. For all its appearance of cultural continuity, for all the liveliness of its art of dance, music and cinema, India is incomplete: a whole creative side has died. It is the price India has had to pay for its British period. The loss balances the intellectual recruitment during this period, political self- (unprecedented in Indian history) and the political reorganization. (*IWC* 113)

The main defect in Naipaul's opinion about India is because he looks India from his own point of view which presents several contradictory pictures of the country. His peculiar vision deprives him of getting a real and genuine view of Indian life as an insider. It becomes clearer when he efficiently describes other social problems which are caused by superstitions, black magic, etc. Naipaul says that Indians are rational about the country's problem, but at times, indulge themselves in the talk of magic, prophecies of astrologers, conservative ideas and the wisdom of auspicious hours: "It seems to be always there in India: magic, the past, the death of the intellect, spirituality annulling the civilization out of which it issues, India swallowing its own tail" (*IWC* 153).

Naipaul's vision of India completely matches with Kipling's view promoted by the West as India has been land of magic, snake charmers and unbreakable superstitions. Even then, the image that Naipaul presents is hard to believe and does not resemble the true picture of India. Akhtar J. Khan sums up his thoughts about V.S. Naipaul's works:

> When we come to analyze the views and visions of Naipaul as projected here, the picture of India appears in a different color, brighter and deeper, of course, with the dark background. In certain places, he also projects complete dark clouds but not, of course, without silver lining. Along with decay, decomposition, frustration, rebellion, fundamentalism and mutinies, he also observes in the intellectual life of India a deep consciousness of wholeness and humanism, growth and restoration. Such perception of India projects his recognition of values, humanism and intellectual development which he had earlier denied to India. (Akhtar 71)

Naipaul finds himself disinherited from all traditions. In *An Area of Darkness*, he confesses of his cultural disinheritance and its personal implications. Naipaul's visit to his ancestral village and meeting his relatives there is not a good experience. Thus, he does not succeed in establishing any meaningful connection between him and his Brahmin ancestors in India. Naipaul's anger, frustration and outburst derive from his cultural disinheritance and it causes an agonizing self-resulting in no stable identity and a strange homecoming.

Naipaul has observed many unpleasant things and activities performed by Indian people. He is shocked to see the civic sense of Indians when one of the beautiful tourist spots of Srinagar, which has to be used with care but its lower slopes are used as latrine by Indian tourists. He is also surprised to see a group of three women defecating, have no shame in exposing themselves in such a way. He holds a view that Indians have a very poor sense of sanitation and health science. He witnesses some incidents happening in the country that time where people have annoyed him by defecating at public places. In Madras, the High Court is converted to one of the most popular latrines used by local people and travelers who frequently pass their time and defecate in the gutter there.

And in Goa, people can be seen squatting in a line beside the Mandovi River. They squat close to one another, chat and defecate. Naipaul sadly remarks on this that: "Indians defecate everywhere. They defecate, mostly, beside the railway tracks. But they also defecate on the beaches; they defecate on the hills, they defecate on the river banks; they defecate on the streets; they never look for cover" (*AAD* 70). But on the other hand, he also holds a contradictory view that Indians are the cleanest people in the world. They take a bath every day that is required by their religion and use their left hand in love-making because food is to be taken with the right hand, while Europeans use their right hand to perform all the activities as for love-making, toilet papers and food. Naipaul suggests Indians to learn the science of municipal sanitation from the West. K. Natwar Singh says that Naipaul is fault-finding in every possible thing he could see: "It is Mr. Naipaul's unique achievement to have passed that amount of time in India without meeting a single worthwhile human being. He finds fault in almost everything he sees: the people's habits and their manners, the cities, villages, bureaucracy, railways, army. Even the Taj Mahal is not spared" (Qtd. Rathore Mahanta 43).

Naipaul's misunderstanding of India begins with his first travelogue on India, *An Area of Darkness* and it continues to his second visit to the country, when he has written *India: A Wounded Civilization* that presents a practical account of the nation. He looks at India as a wounded civilization, because it has been attacked by many foreign rulers such as Hunks, Greeks, Bactrians, Parthians, Muslims and Europeans. Naipaul writes how India has been plundered and ruled by various rulers for a long time:

> No civilization was so little equipped to cope with the outside world; no country was so easily raided and plundered, and learned so little from its disasters. Five hundred years after the Arab conquest of Sindh, Moslem rule was established in Delhi as the rule of foreigners, people apart; and foreign rule—Moslems for the first five hundred years, British for the last 150—ended in Delhi only in 1947. (*IWC* ix)

Naipaul reveals about the great histories of the Indian cities and one of them was Vijayanagar—a city of victory, which was established in the fourteenth century, was conquered and demolished by Moslem group in 1565. He describes the destruction of Vijayanagar which was the greatest city in the world at one point in time: "The city was then one of the greatest in the world, its walls twenty-four miles around—foreign visitors have left accounts of its organization and magnificence—and the destruction took five month; some people say a year" (*IWC* 4).

Vijayanagar, Naipaul observes, was established in 1336 by a local Hindu prince, who had been taken to Delhi having been defeated by the Muslims and was forced to adopt Islam and then was sent back to the south as a symbol of Moslem power. But the prince had re-established his identity and announced himself a Hindu again and presented himself as a representative of the Hindu God. But Vijayanagar, which was established as a sign of great resistance, is now only a name as a kingdom of the past and is little remembered. Its bronze sculptures, architectures, landscapes of rock and gravels seem older than they are. Naipaul writes about how destruction and vandalism have degraded the civilization into barbarism: "The Hinduism Vijayanagar proclaimed had already reached a dead end, and in some ways had decayed, as popular Hinduism so easily decays, into barbarism" (*IWC* 6). Many invaders destroyed the man-made mansions, gigantic towered temples and robbed all wealth. Great cities like Tughlakabad, Tata and Vijayanagar lie in ruins. Mosques were built on temples. Glorious relics and monuments were also destroyed. This process of destruction started at the time of Muslims and went on to the British period, Naipaul observes.

Naipaul further presents a subtle and sensitive account of painful experiences of the once colonized people. His realistic approach makes him conscious and critical of failings of the long-established cultures. He has artistically and realistically dealt with the post-colonial themes of alienation, homelessness, mimicry and quest for identity. In *An Area of Darkness*, Naipaul searches for his ethnic roots and this search leads him through a journey to the land of his forefather's three generations back but his journey becomes frustrating, when he finds his roots sterile. It is to believe that Naipaul's exertion as a historical recorder may be due to his inheritance, and his acquired Western mood and thinking faculties, whether in India or in West Indies or in England. As Naipaul moves through the area of darkness, his moral concern and the anguish for India come to the fore. Naipaul's agony is due to his cultural imbalance and shock. His opinions are based on impression rather than information. Amitav Ghosh presents the picture of India as Naipaul sees it:

> After this (an area of darkness) the richly textured islands of his earlier work would disappear, to be replaced by a series of largely interchangeable caricatures of societies depicted as 'half-made' in comparison with Europe.... Predictably, this turn in Naipaul's work proved immensely popular in the West and he was quickly canonized for his indictment of the Third World. It is a measure of his influence that in the West today, travel writers are taken seriously only to the degree in which they are able to replicate the familiar Naipaulean tone of division. (Qtd. Ray 94)

Naipaul also observes many defects and evils in the social system of India. Indians are not in the favor to give up the superstitions which can be replaced by social and social equality. People are orthodox and conservative and they prefer to adhere to blind faith, their deep-rooted customs and tradition, which are no longer in use in the present era. These shortcomings affect country's socio-cultural and economic setup. As a social analyst, Naipaul marks a valid analysis of the crisis of the country: "The Crisis of India is not only political or economic. The larger crisis is of a wounded old civilization that has at last become aware of its inadequacies and is without the intellectual means to move ahead" (*IWC* 8).

Naipaul also writes about Gandhian India, which was, according to him, created in just a short period of eleven years, from 1919 to 1930. Naipaul believes that Mahatma Gandhi presented India in a new way before the world. In those eleven years, India had gone through many new ideas—such as the idea of non-violence, the idea of truth and all this happened during India's struggle for independence. Mahatma Gandhi guided Indians in many helpful ways to get rid of British rule. But Naipaul seems to have a different approach and finds that people of India followed Gandhiji blindly rather than having a rational and logical approach. In *An Area of Darkness*, Naipaul presents an original interpretation of the victories and failures of Gandhiji. He tries to find out the reason behind Gandhi's success before independence and his failures immediately afterwards. Naipaul says that Gandhi had worked upon sleeping civilization but forgot to teach them how to observe. He expresses that Gandhi had created a nation of followers without any leadership and writes, "Gandhi's self-absorption was part of his strength. Without it he would have done nothing and might have even been destroyed. But with this self-absorption there was, as always a kind of blindness" (*IWC* 88-89).

Naipaul is not hopeful about the democratic institutions in India. He thinks that any sort of additional effort at modernization by Indians would directly lead them to confusions that India is already caught in. He observes that Indians follow no ideology which leads them to have no identity further:

> India is without an ideology—and that was the failure of Gandhi and India together. Its people have no idea of the state, and none of the attitudes that go with such an idea: no historical notion of the past, no identity beyond the tenuous ecumenism of Hindu beliefs, and in spite of the racial excesses of British period, not even the beginnings of a racial sense. (*IWC* 155)

Naipaul makes another observation on Indian personality by relating it to "Underdeveloped ego" (*IWC* 90) of an Indian. He cites the idea of Dr. Sudhir Kakar, a psychotherapist at Jawaharlal Nehru University, New Delhi, who has worked both in India and Europe and admits that this "underdeveloped ego" (*IWC* 90) is formed by the "detailed social organization of Indian life" (*IWC* 90). According to Naipaul, Kakar thinks that:

> ...there seems to be a different relationship to outside reality compared to one meet with in the West. In India, it is closer to a certain stage in childhood when outer objects did not have a separate, independent existence but were intimately related to the self and its affective states. They were not something in their own right, but were good or bad, threatening or rewarding, helpful or cruel, all depending on the person's feelings of the moment. (*IWC* 90)

In Naipaul's views, Sudhir Kakar compares the relationships of Indian people to their outside world with a childhood stage of a person when the person establishes the connection to the outside world, through the mother. Similar to a child, Indian people always try to find out the security of life ordered by the society. Indian people can only project themselves by following certain standards set by the society. Namrata Rathore Mahanta sums up Naipaul's observation, which is based on his complete misinterpretation of Sudhir Kakar's idea:

> Quoting Sudhir Kakar, Naipaul concludes that the relationship of Indians to their outside world is more akin to a childhood stage when the person relates to the world through the mother. Similarly, Indians always turn inward, seeking the security of a life ordered by society. Left on his own, the individual is lost because he has no idea of himself. He can project himself only through the security of an ordered society with its rules and rituals. (Rathore Mahanta 59)

Naipaul has tried to analyze the problems and complications of India. In the beginning, of *India: A Wounded Civilization*, he has laid his emphasis as a diasporic writer and his method of enquiry centers round his perception which is clearly different from the deep-rooted Indian perspective. Helga Chaudhary had suggested Naipaul that he should name his book *India: A Wounded Civilization* as: *Hindu India: A Wounded Civilization* (Qtd. Rathore Mahanta 63).

Namrata Rathore Mahanta states that the forced mass conversion during the Mughal period has been overlooked in Naipaul's view of India. Now the people of India serve themselves as Indians and not as Hindus whether they are from any caste, creed or religion but share a common pain. She further supports her view by saying that Naipaul has concentrated on the same pain of people rather than on the difference in sensibilities of Hindu Indian and Muslim Indians.

Naipaul records contemporary India and uses those illustrations as his base material to present facts. He uses the speeches of politicians, and the articles in newspapers as the contemporary version of historical facts and presents them as the validity of his evidence. Fawzia Mustafa holds that: "Naipaul's habit of evaluation still rely upon the historically unreliable synecdochal narrative techniques of reporting, random interviews...clippings...from newspaper accounts...local novels.... Political biographies" (Qtd. Rathore Mahanta 63).

Naipaul views Indian history as dead and as a domain that lacks inspiration and vitality and these features are clearly linked to his own experiences of the Indian society in Trinidad. According to Gordon Rohler, Naipaul's irony enabled him: "To examine his past without only sentimental self-indulgence" (Rohler 139). In connection with Naipaul's irony, William Walsh calls it: "The agent of meditation between experience and vision" (Walsh 76).

Naipaul upholds a view that India firmly needs to waken her in some ways and give up its complacency to deal with new pressures successfully. He holds an opinion that the control of foreign rules, of centuries, made Indian civilization intellectually parasitic on other civilizations:

> To survive in subjection, they have preserved their sanctuary of the instinctive, uncreative life, converting that into a religious ideal; at a more worldly level, they have depended on others for the ideas and institutions that make a country work. The emergency—coming so soon after independence—dramatizes India's creative incapability, its intellectual depletion, its defenselessness, the inadequacy of every Indian's idea of India. (*IWC* 134)

Naipaul brings to India the ideas of Dharma and presents the main concept of Hindu dharma as the correct and authorized way to perform one's duties and regards it as an "elastic concept". In this context, Naipaul recounts one of his meetings with R.K. Narayan, the creator of Malgudi with zest but he complains that he found Narayan's characters in his book far away from the real world. Taking examples from R.K. Narayan's character like Mr. Sampath, Naipaul mocks the Hindu view of life which compels a deeper contemplation before taking any action. Here Naipaul sees a misinterpretation of the ideas of *Karma* and non-violence in Narayan's hero, Srinivas, who is a keen reader of the Upanishads, and misinterprets the word *Nishkaam Karma* as "non-doing". But the Hindu belief behind the word is that a person must perform his duties or doings without thinking benefits or gains. The Gandhian idea of non-violence is also misread by Srinivas as "non-doing and non-interference" (*IWC* 25). Namrata Rathore Mahanta explains as how through analyzing Srinivas, Naipaul analyses the religious philosophy of the other people of India:

> Naipaul finds such an idea of religious surrender as being parasitic and degenerate. In the fate of Srinivas, Naipaul sees the fate of the vast Indian populace that had interpreted its religious philosophy in such a way that the equilibrium of their idea of themselves was maintained. They accepted distress as the divinely ordained predicament of humankind. (Rathore Mahanta 50)

There are many examples as the one cited above observed by V.S. Naipaul, on Hinduism and Hindus. Certain observations are very minute whereas some of them are just passing generalized opinions. According to him, nowhere outside in India caste is the very structure of social survival and in India caste is everywhere. Even Muslims, Christians, and Jews have sub-castes in varying degree. In India, it is the fundamental rhythm because it is sanctioned by scriptures. It is believed that caste system is incompatible with notion of progressive society. Bhikhu Parekh observes:

> Orthodox Hindus defend the caste system on the ground that it is sanctioned by the scriptures. Its critics appeal to the higher principle of the unity of life and oneness of all

> beings that lies at the heart of many of these scriptures, and argue that the caste system is incompatible with it. Both alike judges the systems in terms of the resources of the Hindu culture itself and reach opposite conclusion. (Qtd. Patel 245)

Parekh further adds:

> To take an example from a very differently constituted culture, liberal society considers equality to be one of its central values, and for decades defined it to mean equality of respect and rights. Socialists challenged this on the ground that formally equal rights were empty unless their bearer had the resources to exercise them equally effectively, and that an adequate definition of equality should include a board equality of these resources. Liberals argued that Socialists were over extending the meaning and even subverting the idea of equality by smuggling in the very different idea of social justice; sociologist rejoined that they were only giving it a coherent and realistic meaning and accused liberals of disingenuously restricting the term within the narrow confines of the capitalist society. (Qtd. Patel 245)

However, the caste system is generally established and it goes on widening into sub-castes and branches. Caste system cannot be understood fully apart from Hinduism. In Hinduism, *Karma* and *Dharma* are the twin essentials as *Karma* provides according to one's deeds in a previous life and *Dharma* demands that one should accept one's condition without complaint.

Naipaul opines that India is a country now populated also with Muslims, Christians, Sikhs, Parsees, Jews, Jains, Buddhist, Aryasamajist, etc.—people other than Hindus. Hindus are divided into many castes and communities. That is why, it has been argued that it is not an organized religion in the way that other religions are. It is only a cluster of communities and that is why it could not stand against the invasion of Muslims. Hindus don't have a collective feeling; they can't be united. They quarrel among themselves over petty issues. Hindus are divided into various sub-castes, creeds and sects. This happens because people have rebelled and degenerated into sects.

In the same critical-objective way, Naipaul also records his ideas of the farm workers and laborers of North Bihar and Rajasthan. Bihar which was called "the cultural heartland" of India remained plagued with poverty and sufferings for more than two decades after India got freedom. People have made up their mind to accept all the sufferings and cruelties. Naipaul marks his impressions about Rajasthan also in the same way. He cites two examples of how development has come to this state. Naipaul surveys dams and irrigation schemes. Second thing which he notices is the peasants using the latest agriculture techniques. Electricity is also available in the village, which is a sign of development in the city, but the women are excluded from all such advancements. They are kept under their veils when a higher officer starts his important discussion. Bundi as a center of art has its own school of painting, though it has lost all its charm and vitality. And the castle of Bundi, which is in a condition of dilapidation, has nothing to be done by the people of Bundi. Namrata Rathore Mahanta points out the helplessness of the people who are totally dependent on the authority for any municipal decision, as recorded in Naipaul's narrative:

> The people of Bundi saw themselves as being completely dependent on the power of the authority and did nothing more than putting up an elaborate show of their deference to authority. They were "less amenable to the commissioner's ideas". They were secure in their condition and the only passion that could move them was a passion for honour. Apart from this, they could not be moved to any form of action. Their world was lost and in order to maintain that old equilibrium, they had "retreated to their last, impregnable defense: their knowledge of who they were, their caste, their *karma*, their unshakable place in the scheme of things". (Rathore Mahanta 50-51)

Naipaul further maintains that during the Emergency, people were against the Prime Minister Indira Gandhi without any true idea of revolution. All protesters were under the illusion of *Karma* and *Dharma*. They thought this revolution will mark new beginnings but they did not know about invisible curtain on reality. Naipaul finds that even in the phase of the Emergency, the illusion of the old equilibrium survived. But this time there appears a change in R.K. Narayan's journey from *Mr. Sampath* to *The Vendor of Sweets*. Naipaul observes about R.K. Narayan:

> In the 1930s, before Independence, that Narayan had established his fictional world: the small pacific South Indian town, little men, little schemes, the comedy of restricted lives and high philosophical speculation, real power surrendered long ago to the British rulers, who were far away and only dimly perceived. With independence; however the world had grown larger around Narayan. People had come closer; men were required to be bigger. To Narayan himself had come recognition and foreign travel. (*IWC* 28)

The Vendor of Sweets, like *Mr. Sampath* recaps the subject of the previous book, Naipaul observes: "there is a venture into the world of doing, and at the end there is a withdrawal (*IWC* 28). It is a story about Jagan, who is a sweet-vendor and a rich man. He is a pious Hindu and a blind follower of Gandhi who does not cheat on his customers but he is not fair with the government of his country. He does not pay sales tax. He has no idea of independence and self-governance. His idea of nation is limited as his idea of Gandhi. Naipaul says that Jagan would have surely paid sales tax if Gandhiji had ever mentioned about it anywhere. Naipaul further asks:

> Was Jagan then a freedom fighter, concerned about the political humiliations of his country, or was he only the disciple of a holy man, in the old Hindu tradition? Hindu morality, centered on the self and self-realization, has its own social corruptions: How many Jagans exist who, conscious only if their Gandhian piety, their personal virtue have mocked and undermined the independence for which say they have worked! But Narayan doesn't raise the point. He only makes the joke about Gandhi and the sales tax; he is on Jagan's side. (*IWC* 29)

According to Naipaul, the old equilibrium has shattered with the entry of Jagan's son with a woman, apparently his wife, who is half-Korean, half-American. However, shattering of the old equilibrium could not be seen as negative. It is a positive beginning. Naipaul points out:

> With Independence and growth, chaos and a loss of faith, India was awakening to its distress and the cruelties that had always lain below its apparent stability, its capacity simply for going on.... The old equilibrium had gone.... But out of this chaos, out of the crumbling of the old Hindu system, and the spirit of rejection, India was learning new ways of seeing and feeling. (*IWC* 38)

Naipaul argues that Indian civilization is a wounded one and convinces the readers that India has always been under change but irony is that change is not driven by convictions and locatedness time and space. Indians always believe in *Karma* and this *Karma* never allows them to conduct self-examination. When tragedy strikes people find refuge in *Karma* (after effect of previous action) and thinks of *Moksha* (redemption). An Indian never believes in self, but reacts to time and space. Naipaul regards Indian intellectual life as short and now, under depletion. It has borrowed everything from alien place, he observes.

Naipaul's concerns in *India: A Wounded Civilization* is not confined to the identity crisis and degeneration caused under Mughal conquest. He analyses various maladies that have reduced India's once brilliantly beautiful past to its gloomy and depressing present. Naipaul's response to the destruction of Babri Masjid is in tune with Naipaul's view in *India: A Wounded Civilization.* He holds a view about Hindu India that they invited conquests and finds that the present has led to the creation of a new sense of identity upon the Hindu past. He considers the demolition of Babri Masjid as a very small part of the vast change in the Hindus' idea of themselves and as an effort to recover their identity of the pre-Islamic period. According to Naipaul, religion has, fortunately or unfortunately, been a part and parcel of every Indian and could have been the starting point of an intellectual discussion in India.

Naipaul realizes that Indian civilization is in an advanced state of decay and that it lacks creativity and drives and is obsessed by symbols, caste and class, and in short, lacks historical self-. He maintains that Indians invited plunders and arbitration of foreigners. He remarks on the widespread apathy and fatalism that makes people ignore even in their immediate environment and notes their utter loss of aesthetic sensibilities of a rich tradition that was built centuries ago. His expressions show his deep concern India. If there is loathing, there is also love on his part, even if it is not the most recognizable kind that one can accentuate.

WORKS CITED

Chaudhary, Helga. "V.S. Naipaul's Changing Vision of India: A Study of *An Area of Darkness* and *India: A Wounded Civilization*". *Literary Half Yearly*, 23, No. 1, January 1982. pp. 111-14.

Harit, Satish K. "V.S. Naipaul and Indian Psyche", Mohit K. Ray (ed.), *V.S. Naipaul: Critical Essays,* Vol. II. Atlantic Publishers and Distributors, 2002. pp. 76-84.

Iyer, N. Sharada. "Naipaul's *India—An Area of Darkness*". Mohit K. Ray (ed.), *V.S. Naipaul: Critical Essays,* Vol. II. Atlantic Publishers and Distributors, 2002. pp. 85-95.

Kakar, Sudhir. *The Inner: A Critical Study of Psycho Analytical Study of Childhood and Society in India*, New Delhi: OUP, 1978.

Khan, Akthar J. *V.S. Naipaul: A Critical Study*, Creative Books, 1988.

Mustafa, Fawzia. *V.S. Naipaul.* Cambridge University Press, 1995.

Naipaul, V.S. *An Area of Darkness*, Picador, 2002.

Naipaul, V.S. *India: A Wounded Civilization*, Picador, 2002.

Patel, Vasant S. *V.S. Naipaul's India: A Reflection.* Standard Publishers, 2005.

Rathore Mahanta, Namrata. *V.S. Naipaul: The Indian Trilogy.* Atlantic Publishers and Distributors, 2004.

Ray, Mohit K. (ed.), *V.S. Naipaul: Critical Essays*, Vol. II. Atlantic Publishers and Distributors, 2002.

Rohler, Gordon. "The Ironic Approach: The Novels of V.S. Naipaul", *The Island in Between*, Ed. Louris Jamea, London, Oxford University Press, 1986. pp. 139-41.

Walsh, William. *V.S. Naipaul.* Edinburgh and Boyd, 1973.

5

The Outsider's Perspective

V.S. Naipaul is an enthusiastic traveler. His travel writings exhibit his observation and concern for the weak, sympathy for the sufferers and his minute evaluation of manners, physical surroundings and development of countries he visit. As V.S. Naipaul has already been described as an expatriate, many of the ideas and themes like the idea of a global citizen's independence and experience of rootlessness which spring from his Diasporic existence find expression in his non-fictional works. His trilogy on India explores the sensibility and identity of an expatriate in the setting of the country of his forefathers. Mallikarjun Patil brilliantly makes a case for Naipaul's greatness as a travel writer:

> V.S. Naipaul, one of the greatest Caribbean writers in English, has been a great novelist and travel writer. V.S. Naipaul, a great Trinidadian writer of Indian descent, wrote many splendid and excellent novels and collection of essays. As a novelist, he is an international figure and exceptional in that matter.... There is no other writer in the Third World who can excel him in quality as well as quantity. His dozen of Novels and two dozens of non-fictional works, no doubt, can make the general readers wonderstruck. (Qtd. Ray 143)

V.S. Naipaul, the 'grandson of a village' of Uttar Pradesh, visits India in February 1962, for the first time and travels many places including Uttar Pradesh, Madras, and Kashmir. Naipaul records his experiences and impressions of India, in his Indian trilogy, particularly in *An Area of Darkness* and provides minute details of his observations. The over-crowded roads, pavements and bazaars fill him with awe and he gets shocked to see the hectic scenes of Mumbai. He tells that as soon as he lands at Bombay port, he faces coolies, fellow travelers, policemen, beggars and others. He feels that: "To be in Bombay was to be exhausted. The moist heat sapped energy and will, and some days passed before I decided to recover my bottles" (*AAD* 9-10).

Naipaul expresses his frank opinion about India and its people and declares Indians as greedy and ignorant. The most striking to the eye for Naipaul, before he can penetrate into the psyche of India, is his visual impression. He sees the country full of dirt, dust, starved masses, sick people and poor beggars. Indian poverty, commented on throughout the travelogue, is for Naipaul an enormously painful experience that he goes through, in the country during his visits. His vivid descriptions of people squatting in the streets and of dirty and decrepit beggars craving for alms create a typical picture of Indian environment. According to him, "India is the poorest country in the world" (*AAD* 41). To support his assertion, Naipaul cites his dear Hindi novelist Premchand who states that even beggars of that time leave their doors "empty-handed" (*AAD* 41). Naipaul asserts in this connection: "That, indeed, is our poverty: not the fact of beggary, but the beggars should have to go from our doors empty-handed. This is our poverty, which in a hundred Indian short stories in all the Indian languages drives the pretty girl to prostitution to pay the family's medical bills" (*AAD* 41).

Naipaul highlights that beggary has its special position in India and cannot be judged from a European perspective. Beggars have a secure position within the society and they are inseparable elements of India. But eminent critics of the same time, like C.D. Narasimhaiah and Anniah Gowda gets upset at Naipaul's half-hearted approaches and prejudices towards India and regard his first book on India, *An Area of Darkness*, is not a true record of the country. They hold a view that Naipaul tries to make his travelogues interesting and attractive for the Western reading public and that is why he adopts faults-finding approach in his travelogues. D.D. Maini thinks that Naipaul comes to India in a mood of mockery with a belligerent attitude towards the country and expresses his feelings: "Naipaul appears to have little respect for, and less understanding of, the vast sociological and psychic changes now underway in India" (Maini, Qtd. Ray 153).

The Indian part of Naipaul's identity is completely suppressed by his Western self and he witnesses everything in the county to which he comes across, covering his eyes with the Western lenses. He observes closely, the writers, religious men, social workers, reformers, law, press, government and the social, economic, and political scenario of the country. In *India: A Wounded Civilization*, he declares without hesitation, the doom of democracy in India: "The dismantled institutions—of law and press and parliament—cannot simply be put together again; it has been demonstrated that freedom is not an absolute in independent India" (*IWC* 155).

Naipaul also comments on the main political parties of the country and notices Congress as the best political party that serves the interest of Muslims in India. One of the narrators of Naipaul, Amir, a member of the Legislative Assembly representing the Congress party, is associated with the party for three or four years. His father belongs to the Muslim League, which is an opposition party to Congress in the 1930s and 1940s. Naipaul points out: "But now in India the Congress was the party that best served the interest of Muslims; and, in a further twist, as a politician Amir used the title, Raja of Mahmudabad, to establish the link with his forebears, and to give a 'focus of identification' to the local Shia and Muslim community" (*MMN* 434).

In the connection of Hindus and Muslims, Naipaul comments on the relations between India and Pakistan as these two countries are regarded as the adversaries. There have been situations of wars between the duo, as in 1965 and 1971. The war of 1971 with Pakistan is a blot in the Hindu-Muslim relationship. According to Naipaul, every Muslim of India has a soft corner for Pakistan, and they have been more loyal to Pakistan than India, since the time of partition. The pre-independence election already proves it. Naipaul supports his assertion when only one Muslim nationalist seat is won by Congress and all in other Muslim constituencies the Muslim League candidates win election. Even the partition of India has not changed the situation. Naipaul painfully observes: "The Indo-Pakistan war of 1971 was a watershed not only in Muslim lives, but also in Hindu Muslim relationship.... Here was India playing a decisive role in the subcontinent. Every Muslim had a soft corner in his heart for Pakistan" (*MMN* 432-33).

According to Naipaul, there has always been communal disharmony between Hindus and Muslim and as a result of this communal disharmony, there have always been adverse reactions. The communal riots take place very often. In 1969, on the day of Gandhi Jayanti, 2nd October, there were such riots in all over Gujarat. In this year, the city of Ahmadabad was under fire. Such communal riots happen frequently. Again in 1989 the similar incident happened. For such communal riots, Naipaul blames not only the common mass but maulvis and religious leaders also. They provoke people, break the law and order and divide people into groups. He maintains that people have become non-secular and many non-secular slogans are put on the walls like 'LIBERATE HUMANITY THROUGH ISLAMS' (*MMN* 33) and notices a printed slogan in tall black letters on a white wall near Mohammed Ali Road, a Muslim area of downtown Bombay. Naipaul narrates the scenario:

> Mohammed Ali Road had a reputation. It was main thoroughfare of the Muslim area of downtown Bombay. The area was spoken of as a 'ghetto', and it was so often in the news in, such worrying ways, that people tended to use newspaper language to describe it. It was where communal riots could begin and, having begun, could spread like fire. (*MMN* 33)

Naipaul has recorded many instances when the Hindu-Muslim riots may break out any time. Anwar, a young man who lived in the Mohammed Ali Road reports that during the last World Cup One-Day Cricket match at Bangalore between

India and Pakistan there have been communal riots in Baroda after Pakistan had lost a cricket match to India. Anwar narrates painfully:

> You have these clashes between children which turn into blood feuds with adults, and I feel helpless to do anything about it. Fights take place between neighbors all the time. When they are Hindus and Muslims—Hindus are in a minority here—it turns into a communal riot. It gets very bad during cricket matches. When there was the World Cup last year—the one-day cricket matches—people became nervous about the India-Pakistan matches. But then neither India nor Pakistan went into the finals. When Pakistan lost the first semi-final to Australia, the Hindus went wild, and they threw stones and broke the asbestos roofs of the huts. (*MMN* 37-38)

Naipaul further states about another political party—Shiv Sena, a powerful local political party in Bombay, known for its regional pride involved in some peace-breaking activities. These people break open Muslims' shops and are involved even in extortion, Naipaul says. There is a riot affected area near Bombay known as Bhiwandi, where communal riots take place usually. Mr. Patil, the narrator of Naipaul describes the clashes between the two communities.

There is a place called Bhiwandi, about 25 kilometers away from here. When India lost a cricket match to Pakistan, they used to let off crackers in the market place, the Muslim there. When I was small I could do nothing about it. But now I can't bear it. There used to be groups of Muslims who used to come over from Bhiwandi to Thane here. The local people were so full of resentment against those Muslims that they had clashes with them in 1982, and they broke open the Muslim shops and sold towels for two rupees. The Muslim shops have come back now, but they live in fear, the Shiv Sena is very powerful. I will tell you: the Muslims even give donations to Shiv Sena (*MMN* 27).

With reference to the disharmony between Hindus and Muslims, Naipaul also comments on the role of police during such riots. He says that the role of police is very strange and they can be bribed for any work that one wishes to do illegally as for example—to kill a cow in public by giving a bribe to a policeman. Anwar narrates this situation sarcastically:

> I have no confidence in the police. I will tell you. You can't kill cows in public here—there an abattoir you have to take your cows to. But you can pay a policeman, and kill a cow in Public. When goats have to be sacrificed at the festival of Id, most Muslims take goats to the abattoir to have them slaughtered. But there are some local hoods who insist on killing the goats in public. It's a macho act, to challenge the police. When the public come, the hoods say: "If you interfere, you won't leave here alive." (*MMN* 40)

According to Naipaul, the police provide help in breaking the law and order in the society. The police are corrupt. This shows Naipaul's close readings of Indian police, reading of Hindus, Hindu-Muslim conflicts, and Islam.

Naipaul finds many mutinies in India. These mutinies are in the form of riots or movements. One of the movements observed by Naipaul is the anti-Brahmin movement led by Periyar Ramaswami. Periyar is a Tamil word which means a sage or a wise man. He is a known prophet from South and is an atheist and rationalist. He ridicules the Hindu gods and also says that Hindus have copied their gods from the gods of ancient Egypt, Greece, Persia and Chaldea. There is another narrator of Naipaul named Sadanand who narrates the humiliation of non-Brahmins which is like an untouchability in a different form. He tells that in a Brahmin hotel when his brother dips a brass tumbler in the bowl of water and starts drinking water, the proprietor gets very angry with him and shouts at him because non-Brahmins are not allowed to take water themselves. Sadanand also talks of anti-Hindu agitation of 1938, and how Congress Government is opposed by people when they propose to introduce Hinḍi compulsorily in the schools. There is an agitation started by Tamil scholars and by Periyar and his group throughout the state. Periyar explains the importance of English which, according to Sadanand, downgrades the culture and society of the state. Sadanand narrates in this connection:

> He explained how Hindi was going to eliminate English, and how this elimination of English was going to be a disadvantage for Tamil Nadu. Tamil would become secondary to Hindi in the course of time. Once the language got downgraded, everything related to the culture and the society would also be downgraded. Everybody in the audience agreed with this. (*MMN* 268)

Naipaul updates that this ideal of Periyar was followed by the other young and middle-aged followers. One of them was Annadurai, who later started the caste-based party DMK and got it to the victory in the state election in 1967. The party remains in power for some years but the opinions related to the DMK Government are varying. The experience under such an ideology is not always good, according to Naipaul. He narrates the changing position of the DMK Government across the state that time:

> The DMK government was very good at the beginning. But power corrupts, and the Brahmins are intelligent people. They have their own means of diluting the devotion of these people to social reforms. They promise things from the centre in Delhi—return for which they want concession locally. They are preeminent in the cultural field. There again they tone down the efforts and intensity put forward by the state government. (*MMN* 274-75)

Naipaul further speaks about the people like Palani who are against the use of institutions like the ancient temples of the city, to create caste distinction among people. According to him, such types of views provoke the people of one caste, community or a religion and are very harmful for the social structure of a society. He further states that allowing only Brahmins to take water from the tank and use it in the *sanctum sanctorum* is not just. Prohibition to people of other caste except Brahmins is partial. Mr. Palani answers when Naipaul asks him about the Mylapore temple:

> I would like Mylapore temple and tank to continue and uphold their architectural and cultural part of our heritage. But still at the same time I am against these institutions being used to create differences among people. They say that Brahmins alone can take water from the tank and use it in the Sanctum Sanctorum. Only Brahmins can go there. People have tried to go into the Sanctum in other places, but they have been prevented by law. About 10 years back, Mr. Karunanidhi, the DMK chief-minister then—he's chief minister again now, after the election introduced a law that non-Brahmins should be entitled to become priests. The Brahmins took the matter up, and the law was struck down by the Supreme Court of India on the grounds that Hindu law as it is today required priests to be Brahmins. (*MMN* 274)

In this way, according to Naipaul, the caste-community politics threatens the spirit of secularism by provoking and pitting one caste or community against another.

Naipaul further states that, there are so many kingdoms and so many rules in India. The state of Karnataka itself is a new creation and is a linguistics state. This land is regarded as one of the sacred lands but there is not any political history behind it. Religious myths about the state exist in every part of this landmass except colonial Goa. Those myths are about gods and the heroes of the epics. There are many stories and fables related to the state and that is what people see and feel at their heart. While visiting Karnataka, Naipaul finds buses full of young men, who are in black tunics and black lower cloths. They look like as they are on a holiday excursion. The young men in black are on a pilgrimage to shrine honoring Ayappa. Naipaul pens his observation about the syncretic faith that the pilgrim follow, during his visit to Bangalore:

> When I got to Bangalore I learned that the men in Black were on a pilgrimage. They were going to a shrine in the southernmost state of Kerala. The shrine honored Ayappa, a Hindu ruler and saints of days gone by. The pilgrimage was essentially a Hindu affair; but the pilgrims to Ayappa

> were also required, in an unlikely way, to do honour to Vavar, an Arab and a Muslim, who had been a friend and ally of Ayappa's. (*MMN* 169)

This Ayappa pilgrimage is an example of Hindu-Muslim unity. Naipaul further talks about other Gods in Hinduism and says that there are many gods in this religion and one of them is Ganesh or Ganpati. V.S. Naipaul is told by Mr. Patil, the Shiv Sena area leader in Thane, about the confidence they get from Ganpati. Mr. Raote, another leader of Shiv Sena, has also said that he gets his confidence from religion in the larger sense, rather than from Ganpati in specific and continues that Ganpati is not merely a God. Ganpati festival is celebrated generally in Maharashtra. But recently it has got importance in various parts of Gujarat also. Earlier only Maharashtrians used to celebrate the festival. Naipaul recalls what Mr. Raote says:

> He is not a special diety. Everything in India begins with Ganpati or Ganesh. No Hindu puja starts without him. The religion we have is from childhood. It is part and parcel of our life. No Hindu family will give up the morning puja. We have a special garment for the puja. Religion definitely gave us confidence. It built our character. (*MMN* 50)

Naipaul claims that in Maharashtra, Shiv Sena is very popular. It is a political party which strongly believes in Hinduism. Naipaul visits the room of Mr. Ghate, a Shiv Sena official. The area at the front of Ghate's room is the office and it has the big flitted cupboard. Mr. Ghate feels sorry for the extravagance, and explains that he bought the cupboard last year because he had to deal with large amount papers because of his Sena's work. Naipaul observes:

> There were more than papers behind the glass doors of the cupboard. On a top shelf were tumblers and plates in plastic and stainless steel. On other shelves were photographs, and a gold colored plaque with the new Marathi slogan of the Sena. I had heard about: *Say it with pride: 'I'm a Hindu'*. The Sena, as it had become more powerful, was trying to be less regional. It was appealing now to a more general Hindu sentiment, and some people found this as worrying

as its earlier call of Maharashtra for the Maharashtrians. (*MMN* 74)

Naipaul observes that people consider Brahmins as the most important or the valuable caste or community among Hindus. There is a belief that if someone is born and brought up in priestly community then that they do not require anything more in their lifetime. One of the narrators of Naipaul named Pravas tells that his grandfather had been a priest. He used to chant Mantras and was an old classical ritualistic purohit and his profession was to perform rituals. Pravas points out in this connection:

> The internal factor is that the priestly community was born and brought up with the psychology that they didn't expect more. It's so much part of the internal system that it's gone down to the folk level. The lord Vishnu has two wives—Lakshmi, the goddess of wealth, and Saraswati, the goddess of wisdom. The two wives would naturally be at loggerheads—a depiction of the fact the intellectual life seldom goes with wealth: you have to choose one of them. So, by a combination of circumstances, this priestly class didn't look for riches and they wouldn't be given riches. A perfect matching of interests. (*MMN* 192)

Naipaul states that Brahmins are expected to live the life of purity and piety. He also states that among Hindus eating is taken as a sacred activity and tells that there is a fixed time for eating with a certain amount of food. Addition to it, he says that Hinduism, being a trinity-based religion, has three positions for everything, and food is also of three types—*Sattvik, Rajasik, Tamasik*. People of higher castes are not allowed to eat food cooked by someone of lower caste and there are rigid prescriptions about the timings of eating, direction of eating, who serves it and how much to eat. With the old and orthodox ideals of Hinduism, the food is exactly contrary to that of Muslim food which is supposed to promote violence. Naipaul writes about the food and its types, clearly stating the inclusion of grains and vegetables in each category:

> Hinduism is a trinity-based religion—there are three options for everything. So food was of three kinds—*sattvik, rajasik, tamasik*. *Sattvik* foods encouraged intellectual pursuits, clarity of mind, purer thoughts. *Sattvik* food is very light—most grains, a certain amount of clarified butter, the lighter vegetables. *Rajasik* food is work oriented. (*MMN* 193)

According to Naipaul, along with Hinduism and Muslim religion, there is also a European Christianity in India and it is mainly visible in old Goa. History in Goa is simple to Naipaul. Naipaul writes about the history of Goa:

> Historical names were on that road down through Karnataka. Bijapur was one such name. It was the name of a Muslim kingdom, established almost at the same time as Portuguese in Goa (Goa had, in fact, been taken away from Bijapur). The name was associated in my mind not with Goa or Old Goa but with a fine Persian-influenced 17th century school of miniature painting: the very name brought the faces and the postures and the special colors and costumes to my mind. But how did Bijapur fit into the history of the region? What were its dates, its boundaries? Who were its rulers and enemies? It was hard to carry all of that in the mind: I would have to look it up in the books, and even then (though I would learn that it had lasted two centuries) I would get no more than the bare bones of dates and rulers. Its achievement, after all, hadn't been that great; there was nothing in its history to catch the mind, as there was in the art (and the architecture, from my reading: a certain kind of dome). And so that name of Bijapur and the other historical names on the road south, were like random memories in an old man's mind. (*MMN* 168-69)

Thus, Naipaul has analyzed different religions, sects and sectarian groups of India. He opines that, in a purely Muslim country people might have been less worried about their faith, but in India, because it is a Hindu-dominated country, that is why Muslims are more threatened. When Naipaul is in Lucknow, near the end of his trip, Rashid tells him about the most worrying threats when a man from Bangalore has filed a petition in the court to ban the Koran on the ground that it preaches sedition. Naipaul explicates, in this connection:

> Near the end of my time in Lucknow Rashid told me what the most worrying recent threats had been. There was the man from Bangalore who had petitioned the court to ban the Koran in all its languages and editions in India, on the grounds that the Koran preached sedition. The petition was a form of provocation, and should not have been taken seriously. Instead, Rashid said, the judge, a woman, rather too legalistically agreed to consider the petition. This caused rioting. The petition was thrown out later by another judge, who ruled that the Koran, like the Bible, was 'a basic document', and could not be the subject of that kind of legal petition. (*MMN* 422)

Naipaul affirms that the root of such a threat lies in the pre-independence history of India. At the outset itself Muslims in India are believed to have different interests from the rest of the communities. The principal idea of communal representation is defended on the grounds that Muslims are suppressed by the non-Muslim community and the climax is a demand of separate Pakistan by Muslim league. The fruits of the separate nation of the Pakistan are still to be viewed in India in the form of communal disharmony or breaking out of communal riots. Discussing the relationship between Hindu and Muslim community, he points out the dispute of a Babri mosque in Ayodhya built on Ram Janam Bhoomi and considers it still a burning issue. Ayodhya, is regarded as an important and pious city, the birthplace of Lord Rama, the hero of *Ramayana*. Hindus argue that after invasion the Muslims builds a mosque on the site of Rama's birthplace. When India becomes independent, Hindus claims the site again. He adds that since 1949, the mosque has been closed because of the fear of communal disharmony. After a Hindu petition for permission to pray, the locks are opened. Hindus are in possession of this place. There have been riots, people have been killed but the dispute is still going on. The mosque has been demolished in

1992 and the issue has been settled by Allahabad High Court in 2011. Naipaul sums up:

> Then there was the affair of a mosque in the town of Ayodhya, 300 miles away, which the Hindus have turned into a temple. Ayodhya was important, even sacred to Hindus. It was the birthplace of Lord Rama, the hero of the Ramayana; and there were Hindus who said that after the invasion the Muslims had built a masque on the site of Rama's birthplace. With independence, Hindus wished to claim the site again. In 1949, Rashid said, the mosque was closed down, because of the danger of rioting. Then, four years ago or so ago, there had been a development. A Hindu petitioned the district judge for permission to pray there. The permission was allowed. The locks of the place were opened; Hindus took possession and were still in possession. There had been riots; people had been killed; the bitter squabble was still going on. (*MMN* 422-23)

Naipaul terms Babri mosque and the Kashmir as the ever burning issues responsible for communal disharmony or a threat to secularism in India. The mosque at Ayodhya stands demolished under the security of armed police, but Kashmir is a different type of problem; the condition has entered into a "stand-still" agreement between India and Pakistan and both countries want to sort out the problem of its possession. B.G. Gokhale points out in this connection:

> Kashmir posed a problem of a different magnitude. The state had entered into a "Stand Still" agreement with the two dominions of India and Pakistan as it wanted time to consider the problem of its accession. The state has an area of 84,4471 sq. miles and borders on India, Pakistan and Soviet Union. Pakistan was virtually interested in forcing the Maharaja to accede to it and committed breeches of the standstill agreement by obstructing the flow of civil supplies to the state. This was followed by a large scale invasion of state by members of the north-western frontier tribe aided by the Pakistani army led by prominent officers of that army who ostensibly were "on leave". In October, 1947 the

> situation became very critical for raiders had looted and burnt their ways to Srinagar, the Capital. The Maharaja then appealed to India for military assistance and signed the instrument of accession where upon Indian troops were flown to Kashmir to fight back invaders. The Maharaja was supported in his action by the political leaders of Kashmir and Indian government had expressed his desire to let the people of Kashmir ratify the accession of their state to India through a plebiscite after the state was cleared of all invaders and peace restored to it. On the 31st December, 1947, India lodged a complaint with the security council of the United Nations charging Pakistan with aggression against Kashmir which was the part of the territory of the dominion of India by virtue of its accession...Pakistan has been supporting the puppet government of so-called Azad of "Free" Kashmir and its troops still occupy nearly a third part of the state's territory. (Qtd. Patel 287)

Thus, according to Naipaul, Kashmir is one of the burning problems, unresolved so far but he thinks that the issue of mosque is not a religious problem but rather it is a political one. It is only the political leaders of both the communities who provoke people to fight with each other and the people appear to be interested in fighting rather than earning their livelihood. The poor can't afford to go so long without work. But the moulvis and priest provoke them. It seems to be the vested interest of political leaders to keep the issue unresolved, he opines.

In the context of religion in India, Naipaul further tells about Vishwa Nath, who is the editor of a famous magazine and is not a religious man at all. He believes that "Upanishads are just a play of words" (*MMN* 487) and "religion is the great curse of mankind" (*MMN* 488), which has killed people. To Vishwa Nath, the oldest profession is not prostitution, it is the priesthood. Vishwa Nath makes a thought-provoking statement concerning the same:

> I think religion is the greatest curse of mankind. It has killed more people, destroyed more property, than any other

> things. Even today—Northern Ireland, the Middle East. Hindus, Muslims, Sikhs, all fighting each other in India. The oldest profession is not prostitution. It is the priesthood.... In India this concern was like a wish to preserve the old social order; and perhaps, like the iconoclasm, it came out of some personal need. (*MMN* 488)

Vishwa Nath's belief shows that common people are more interested in earning their livelihood for feeding their family. But the provocations are responsible for killing people and destroying property. The demolition of the mosque at Ayodhya takes place on December 6, 1992 which defames the republic of India, the *Times of India* notes in its editorial:

> The worst was feared in Ayodhya: and the worst has come to pass. The disputed Babri Masjid structure has been razed to the ground. Despite solemn promises made to the Supreme Court, the Kalyan Singh government and the leaders of the Sangh parivar failed to prevent this gross act of Vandalism. The failure reveals their inability or unwillingness or both to operate within the confines of the constitutions. No matter how much they try to explain away the destruction of the Mosque, the fact remains that in the eyes of the nation they have effectively placed themselves outside the rule of law. The BJP, which has in power in four states and enjoys considerable influence in several parts of the country, will have to pay a heavy price of its abysmal conduct. In one swift stroke it forfeited its claim to be a party of governance. The nation will be well within its right to ask how it can be entrusted with any responsibility if it lost its nerve with such abruptness during the dramatic development on Sunday. It has invited the charges of unconstitutional behavior...it is not however enough to squarely blame only the *Hindutava* forces for Sunday's developments. The Central government, Parliament, the courts and all those who shape opinion cannot escape their responsibility. Quiet clearly, they were unable to gauge the depth and extent to which the *Hindutava* elements had spread their influence in the body politics. It is otherwise hard to explain the

> behavior of the law and forces and of the administration in Ayodhya. (Qtd. Patel 290-91)

In addition to the above, Naipaul further states that the demolition of the Ayodhya mosque is followed by the dismissal of the 18-months-old BJP Government as the government is dismissed on the night of 6 December 1992 in Uttar Pradesh and the state assembly breaks up officially. Many political parties express their opinion on the issue. One of the major political parties—Congress regarded it "an act of treachery" (Qtd. Patel 296). *The Times of India* reviews:

> "An Act of Treachery", says Congress:
>
> The Congress, today condemned the storming of the disputed structure at Ayodhya by kar sevaks as "an act of treachery".
>
> The party spokesman, Mr. V.N. Gadgil, said the Uttar Pradesh Government had "very inefficiently" handled the situation.
>
> He also condemned the reported manhandling of journalists by the kar sevaks at Ayodhya.
>
> However, the VHP said the damaged caused to the disputed Ayodhya structure was the handiwork of "anti-social elements that had infiltrated the ranks of kar sevaks."
>
> VHP spokesman, Mr. Manoharpuri said that today's incidents in Ayodhya could have been "planned by those who wanted to defame our peaceful movements."
>
> He said the VHP leadership was in no way responsible for the incidents as they had made their intentions clear that the kar seva would be in accordance with the count orders....
>
> As apprehended, all attempts for a peaceful settlement of the dispute and maintenance of the rule had been foiled by the BJP-VHP-RSS combine and UP Government. "We have", Laloo Prasad Yadav, "demanded the resignation of the Narsimah Rao government on grounds of owning moral responsibility for the happenings at Ayodhya."
>
> The Center has failed miserably in discharge of its duties. Alleging that the Congress was "hand in gloves with the

> BJP", the Chief Minister added, the country has plunged into a blind alley. (Qtd. Patel 296-98)

Naipaul further reports that the Babri Masjid issue in present is taken to the Supreme Court by Babri Masjid Action committee. The Supreme Court has removed VHP and Ram Janam Bhoomi Nyas from the list of concerned parties. The hearing and cross examination of witness of Babri Masjid Action Committee are on. Yet 17 parties are to be heard. Common people seem to have almost forgotten the issue and they have become normal, but the political leaders and religious ritualistic priest and moulvis are not ready to give up their bitterness. In fact, they seem to be interested in taking the advantage of the issue in their personal party's favor. Naipaul, however, finds it as an encouraging feature that most people seek the enduring solution of communal problems of the country in strengthening the secular character of India.

Naipaul's *An Area of Darkness* and *India: A Wounded Civilization* both had mixed responses. When Naipaul first came to India, no one could distinguish him from the crowd but he wanted to impose himself as a foreigner. Naipaul remarks in this context:

> And for the first time in my life I was one of the crowds. There was nothing in my appearance or dress to distinguish me from the crowd eternally hurrying into Churchgate station. In Trinidad to be an Indian was to be distinctive. To be anything there was distinctive; difference was each man's attribute. To be an Indian in England was distinctive; in Egypt it was more so. Now in Bombay I entered a shop or a restaurant and awaited a special quality of response. It was like being denied part of my reality. And there was nothing...I felt the need to impose myself, and I didn't know how. (*AAD* 39)

It depresses Naipaul that he could not be recognized as Englishman rather than he is regarded as an Indian student returned from Europe. He finds that his childhood unites him with India but adulthood burdens with reality. However, the healthy changes in Indian literature either in English or in vernaculars and journalism impress him. The magazines like *Woman's Era, Savvy* and *Femina* inform Naipaul about the changes occurring in the nation and their agenda of emancipation and empowerment of women. Naipaul, in one of his meetings with the editors of women's magazines, discovers the tough life of the urban lower-middle class earning women of a family and their day-to-day struggles, when even they have to fight hard to get on suburban trains. Naipaul observes:

> ...she's up at the crack of dawn, about five, to fill the water for the day.... Then she does the morning chores, filling the tiffin carriers for husband and children after giving them tea, breakfast.... Then she's off to work herself. A very long train journey in crowded train, usually. She hardly gets a seat.... She gets off from her office at 5.30 or six. She might first take a bus to the station. Or—this is more harrowing—she might have to take a bus all the way home. There are miles long queues for the bus sometimes.... Before getting to the bus or station would buy her vegetables or whatever she needs.... Then she has to think of the water again. (*MMN* 473)

Thus, the progression of people which Naipaul comes across in *India: A Million Mutinies Now* seems to be closely linked with Naipaul's coming to term with his diasporic status.

Naipaul also observes the position of women in India and discovers that the status of women in the country is not good. Indian society is dominated by men. He has shown no positivism in his portrayal of women in *An Area of Darkness*; rather they are shown to be more retrograde and a part of decaying society. He further talks about issues like bride burning and other different physical and mental tortures for various reasons. Naipaul remarks: "The newspapers had been carrying reports from different parts of the country about Hindu brides being done to death by their husbands' families—often by fire—for not bringing a sufficient dowry or valuable enough gifts. These days a boy's family often required modern gifts, motor-scooters, or expensive electronic goods" (*MMN* 275-76). Naipaul talks about women's exploitation through some social customs like sati, in which a widow immolates herself on her husband's funeral pyre. Many Hindu reformers fought against this social evil. However, the incidents of sati, continues to occur even in post-independence India. This practice reinforces woman's inferiority and generates psychological fear among newly wedded women and even men. Of course, it would lead to deep distress to a widow who sincerely believes that it is her duty to die with her husband. Bhikhu Parekh comments in this connection:

> The practice is of an unknown origin, and in one form or another goes back a long time. During the early days of British rule when it became fairly widespread in some parts of the country, Hindu leaders themselves began to campaign against and created a climate which made it easier for the British to outlaw it in 1829. Incidents of *sati*, however, continued to occur, including in post-independence India, but they were relatively rare and aroused no public concern. The situation changed in 1987 when Roop Kunvar, a well-educated 18 years old Rajput girl married for eight months to a well-educated young man, mounted her husband's funeral pyre watched by thousands of enthusiastic admires. Although accounts of incidents vary, the circumstantial suggests that she was drugged. In any case the incident aroused considerable passion all over India, some strongly supports and others vehemently condemning it. It would seem that large number of Hindus approved of woman's action as judged by the size of public demonstrations in support of it. (Qtd. Parekh 224)

Naipaul cites another important example of the oppression of women with Muslim personal law. Muslims have a special privilege of marrying four times which means they can have four wives at a time and the government cannot interfere in right to Muslims permitting them to divorce their wives with the word "Talaq" spoken thrice. Naipaul observes:

> A Wealthy Muslim lawyer divorced his first wife and married again. He gave the first wife the lump sum stipulated in their Muslim marriage contract. The divorced wife then went to the Indian courts and asked for a monthly maintenance allowance as well from her husband (this

> was how Rashid told the story). After 20 years the case reached the Indian Supreme Court. The judge spoke of the deficiency in Muslim personal law, and granted maintenance to the divorced wife. There was an outcry from Muslim at this interference with their personal law, which was part of their faith; and the Indian government, responding to the protests passed legislation that overturned the decision of the Supreme Court. (*MMN* 423)

Unlike in his earlier two works, in *India: A Million Mutinies Now*, Naipaul portrays women in their socio-economic political backgrounds and has carefully brought out the changes that have occurred in women's lives. He considers Indian women as harbingers of change that has come to India. He explains how Indian women explore the potentials of their surroundings and bring about changes. And this movement has started within the family. It is from that they began to challenge all the social structures of dominance and have begun to negotiate her space in the world in which she inhabits. Women are no longer seen as mothers, whose responsibility is only to bring up their children. Even they have started to build up their own careers, Naipaul, with great hope, observes.

Thus, Naipaul expresses his frank opinion about India and its people. His trilogy is not merely a summary and descriptions of India and its people but it is a very sophisticated personal account of an intimate relationship of a descendant of the Indian emigrant to his mother country. His observation of Indian life is so minute that he looks at every nook and corner of it and no commonest thing relating to it can escape his notice.

WORKS CITED

Naipaul, V.S. *An Area of Darkness*. Picador, 1995.

Naipaul, V.S. *India: A Million Mutinies Now*, Vintage, 1991.

Naipaul, V.S. *India: A Wounded Civilization*, Picador, 2002.

Patel, Vasant S. *V.S. Naipaul's India: A Reflection*, Standard Publishers, 2005.

Patil, Mallikarjun, "India and Nobel Laureate V.S. Naipaul" (ed.), Mohit K. Ray, *V.S. Naipaul Critical Essays*, Vol. II, Atlantic Publishers and Distributors, 2002. pp. 254-66.

6

Conclusion

V.S. Naipaul's literary career is one that is committed to the portrayal of contemporary reality. This commitment is seen in his depiction of India and Hinduism. His upbringing instills in him Hindu rituals at his grandmother's house and the eulogized image of India, which he imbibed at that point, was probably his first link to India and Hinduism. Another influence on him was in the form of religious message introduced through his father's stories.

Isolated due to the displacement, Naipaul examines the world with an open eye and observes a crack between the two worlds in which he inhabited. One was the colonial world of Trinidad and the second, was the old Hindu world of India. The image of India which was constructed in his childhood in the West Indies is destroyed completely when he comes across poverty and impurity of India and feels as a homeless expatriate in the country of his forefathers. He has explored the predicament of the exile, the pain of homelessness and loss of roots with great sensitivity in his Indian Trilogy.

Naipaul's literary engagement with India started with his first book on India, *An Area of Darkness* continued in *India: A Wounded Civilization* and *India: A Million Mutinies Now.* His travel books on India summarize his three visits to the country, in 1962, 1975 and 1988 respectively and provide a very insightful account about the nation and its people. In short, Naipaul's Indian Trilogy is a record of his thoughts, feelings, impressions and views about the country and also the account of the relationship that he develops with the country of his forefathers during these visits. Naipaul's trilogy is not mere a summary and descriptions of India and its people but it is a very sophisticated personal account of an intimate relationship of a descendant of the Indian emigrant to his mother country. In a number of his observations, he appears as complete dissenter where he reveals not only the true state of modern Indian existence, but also his own detached personality, which are truly reflected in his portrayals.

Naipaul's first book on India, *An Area of Darkness* is logically the most emotional and subjective book of the trilogy. It is a semi-autobiographical account of the year (1962) that he had spent in India. The title *An Area of Darkness* refers to darkness of superstition and corruption that was rampant in India. It describes his first visit to the country of his ancestors that was a very emotive experience for Naipaul that he could not remain unmoved. He writes about his experiences in India over span of one year and he does not hesitate to disclose his true feelings and gives reader very melancholic and ironical descriptions of what he observes in the country of his forefathers.

Many of the negative aspects of Indian culture are highlighted and Naipaul seems to see the whole bleakness of the culture at every stage. When he comes to India in 1962, the country was suffering from social and political crises. The economic situation was shattering due to rampant corruption and ineffective governance. From the very beginning it is noticeable that Naipaul is enormously disenchanted with reality that he has to face during his first sojourn in India and often compares India and Trinidad in terms of their colonial past. Consequently, the India of his dreams and the India of his grandfathers is erased forever. Thus, Naipaul's diasporic insecurities begin to represent the first stage of his growth as a diasporic writer. In this book, he has marked the area of pain and degeneration and the area that created unrest in him.

Naipaul second book on India, *India: A Wounded Civilization* marks the second stage in the progression of his engagement with the country. In this book, he exposes the problems of India and identifies the root of all maladies that troubled the country in the forms of repeated invasion and conquests and opines that the traditional knowledge and talent of India vanished with the coming of the British. He further adds that alien institutions ruined traditional institutions systematically. Even after the independence, India could not bring the same talent, knowledge, expertise and craftsmanship into the existence that it had in the past. Naipaul regards Indian Civilization as "As Wounded Civilization", because it has been wounded by the rule of many foreigners such as Hunks, Greeks, Bactrians, Parthians, Muslims and Europeans. Indians were also suppressed and their wealth was plundered in great measures. The central theme of the book revolves around the psyche of the Indian religious experience, the self-absorption of Hinduism and the acceptance of Karmic fate.

Naipaul's third visit to India in 1998 resulted in *India: A Million Mutinies Now.* This book is a record of his travels to the various parts of the country and his efforts to meet people, identify their roots, their ideologies and to get an understanding of the various religious, political and social institutions. Here he takes up the role of a reporter, who painstakingly enumerates what he sees around him. He also records the experiences of various people he meets up and each narrator in the book exposes a special struggle that had led the country to special development. These narrators describe the process of change and development and all these numerous voices from different parts of the country present a complete picture of developing India. In this way, a million voices speak of a million mutinies and revolutions happening in the country. As a result, he looks at the country through the eyes of its people. He has observed India at those places from where regeneration and change have started and has analyzed his own response to this change in the country. He reveals that due to industrialization and green revolution, a new class of rich people is emerging. He further adds that the first time, Indians have an access to university education, but at the same time, he is also annoyed to notice that the criteria of admission to universities are quotas for different classes, not merit. Besides, showing his concern for the living condition of the people of the country, he also comments on the issues like poverty, cleanliness, and vegetarianism and but at the same time, he also appreciates Indian women toiling for their betterment. His observation of Indian life is so minute that he looks at every nook and corner of it. Initially, he shows his displeasure on Indians' superstitions, ignorance, violence, slavish attitude, love for even unhealthy traditions and customs, hardships of life, but later on feels satisfied with the positive changes and progressive attempts initiated by the various groups of the people within the country.

Naipaul admits that Indian society realizes a kind of power generated by its religious rules, clan and rituals and most of its activities are performed as per their religious principles. This acceptance of the author can be supported by the following statement of Sri Aurobindo who had proposed this view of India as a nation:

> Each nation, in Indian concept, is a Shakti or power of the evolving spirit in humanity and lives by the principle which it embodies. India is the Bharata Shakti, the living energy of a great spiritual conception and fidelity to it is the very principle of her existence. For by its virtue alone she has been one of the immortal nations: this alone has been the secret of her amazing persistence and revival. All Asia has always had the spiritual tendency in more or less intensity, with more or less clearness; but in this essential matter India is the quintessence of the Asiatic way of being. (Aurobindo 3)

Naipaul has analyzed his personal responses to India on the basis of his cultural inheritance but above all on the basis of his uncertainty of his roots. He had never felt rooted in Trinidad, where he was brought up to believe that his roots lay in the sacred land of his forefathers. His grandfather had carried with him fairy tales of India as a sacred land but he had not carried tales of Indian poverty with him and never mentioned the reason behind why they shifted to Trinidad as indentured laborers. Thus, his Indian trilogy can be studied as an attempt of a diasporic writer to establish a link with the land of his ancestors by exploring the link between the given idea of homeland and the lived experiences of the same.

Naipaul's three books on India are read to be in a sequence to understand his diasporic status. In this way, his first book on India, *An Area of Darkness* is an attempt to move back from a troublesome reality and comes up as rather a mixed response about the country of his origin. His experiences of India were shocking and full of despair. He vents his emotions when he cannot stand to look at all the squatting people in the dusty street, ragged, scruffy, beggars, and pervasive dirt in the ruins of the long-ago burnt-out glory. Even larger desperateness grows in him with the sad realization that the real India and the India of his childhood imagination are completely different places. Naipaul finds a feeling of dejection in him and writes:

> India had not worked its magic on me. It remained the land of my childhood, an area of darkness; like the Himalayan passes, it was closing up again, as fast as I withdrew from it, into a land of myth; it seemed to exist in just the timelessness which I had imagined as a child, into which, for all that I walked on the Indian earth, I knew I could not penetrate. (*AAD* 274)

In this way, the real India fails to fulfil the vision of the mother country of his imagination. He admits that he had taken the country for granted and confirms that his own lack of understanding has aroused such ideas and reactions but later on, in another visit to India, he makes the following statement on the intellectual development in India: "It was a time of intellectual recruitment. India was set on the way of a new kind of intellectual life; it was given new ideas about its history and Civilization. The freedom movement reflected all of this and turned out to be the truest kind of liberation" (*MMN* 603).

Thus, Naipaul moved gradually towards a better understanding of India and Indian critics also changed their views on him. Through the book *India: A Million Mutinies Now*, he resolves his inner conflicts that were expressed in *An Area of Darkness*. With a mixture of journalistic writings and interviews he explores the India of the latter part of the 20th century through his encounters with religious, political and secular people across the country. He has written a well-researched ethnography combining vigorous journalism and insightful observation of various members of Indian communities and tries to portray the country's growing pains.

Naipaul is the author, whose works are often subject matter of many disputes among the critics. Critics have divided themselves into two opposing parties. Some praise him as one of the most gifted authors of these days, at the same time, others blame him for "racial arrogance" (White 1). He is known as an author, who is either loved and admired or repudiated. Joseph Lelyveld appreciates him for his truthfulness for India and remarks: "The most notable commitment of intelligence that post-colonial India has evoked...he is indispensable for anyone who wants seriously to come to grips with the experience of India" (Qtd. Ray 154). Nonetheless, there is one thing that most of the critics agree on and it is the fact that Naipaul is the master of observation and depiction and always provides his readers with very sophisticated descriptions of what he encounters. His three visits to India, his stay in India for a considerable span of time and his writings about India are a testimony to attraction towards the country. His reactions, howsoever bitter they may be but are a doubtless revelation of his innate and inmost concealed liking for India. His travelogues on India should be accepted as diasporic chronicles that attempt to link the past to the present in ways that lead to a progression in his diasporic mediation with India. His diasporic consciousness is really profound with historical sense, lived experiences, nostalgia, concern for the country of origin and the urge to know it deeply. His trilogy really marks all these attributes of Indo-Caribbean diasporic consciousness.

WORKS CITED

Aurobindo, Sri. *The Foundation of Indian Culture and the Renaissance in India*, Vol. 14. Sri Aurobindo, Birth Centenary Library (Popular Edition), 1972.

Naipaul, V.S. *An Area of Darkness*, London: Penguin Books, 1968.

Naipaul, V.S. *India: A Million Mutinies Now*, Vintage, 1991.

Ray, Mohit K. *V.S. Naipaul Critical Essays*, Vol. II. Atlantic Publishers and Distributors, 2002.

White, Landeg. *V.S. Naipaul: A Critical Introduction*, Macmillan Press, 1975.

Index